Haatchi & *Little B*

The inspiring true story of one boy and his dog

Wendy Holden

Thomas Dunne Books
St. Martin's Press

THOMAS DUNNE BOOKS.
An imprint of St. Martin's Press.

HAATCHI & LITTLE B. Copyright © 2014 by Owen Hopkins
and Wendy Holden. All rights reserved. Printed in the
United States of America. For information, address St. Martin's Press,
175 Fifth Avenue, New York, N.Y. 10010.

www.thomasdunnebooks.com
www.stmartins.com

Library of Congress Cataloging-in-Publication Data

Holden, Wendy, 1961– author.
   Haatchi & Little B : the inspiring true story of one boy and his dog /
Wendy Holden. — First U.S. edition.
      p. cm.
   Includes bibliographical references and index.
   ISBN 978-1-250-06318-2 (hardcover)
   ISBN 978-1-4668-6819-9 (e-book)
   1. Human-animal relationships—England—London. 2. Dogs—
Psychological aspects. 3. Hawkins, Owen, 2005—Health. 4. Genetic
disorders in children—Patients—England—London—Biography. 5.
Haatchi, 2011– I. Title.
   QL85.H65 2014
   636.7—dc23
                                             2014010823

St. Martin's Press books may be purchased for educational, business, or
promotional use. For information on bulk purchases,
please contact Macmillan Corporate and Premium Sales Department at
1-800-221-7945, extension 5442, or write
specialmarkets@macmillan.com.

First published in Great Britain by Bantam Press,
an imprint of Transworld Publishers

First U.S. Edition: July 2014

10 9 8 7 6 5 4 3 2 1

This book is dedicated to those who are different
and to the humans and animals who love them
all the more because of it

Author's Note

ONCE IN A while in life – if we're lucky – we come across those who leave footprints (or pawprints) on our hearts and we are never quite the same again. Haatchi and Little B touched me that way from the moment I was first alerted to their story in late 2012.

There was something about the expressions on both their faces that tugged at my heart and demanded my attention. A lifelong animal lover and a champion of the underdog, I was intensely moved when I read more about their extraordinary experiences and how fate had brought them together. That would make a great book, I told myself.

A few months later, I was unexpectedly asked if I would consider writing that book by Haatchi's adoptive mother, Colleen, and her future husband, Will, the father of Little B. A difficult project I'd been working on for months had fallen through and I was not only available but in need of fresh inspiration. Fate, which had already played such a hand in the experiences of one dog and his boy, drew me to one of the most life-enhancing families I could ever hope to meet.

This is so much more than just a story of unspeakable cruelty to a defenceless animal. It is the redemptive tale of what happens to the spirit in the face of unconditional love, trust and forgiveness. It shows how the worst of human nature can bring out the best.

A remarkable little boy and his family rescued a three-legged dog who then paid them back a thousandfold, changing all their lives for ever.

Their story is far from over, and it will continue to inspire and change the lives of everyone who is lucky enough to meet them in the years to come. I know, because it changed mine. And my heart is covered in their prints . . .

Wendy Holden

'*Adapt yourself to the things among which your lot has been cast and love sincerely the fellow creatures with whom destiny has ordained that you shall live.*'

Marcus Aurelius

Prologue

*L*IFTING HIS HEAD, *he sniffed the chill night air with his wet black nose. He tried to move but the pain was too severe, so he slumped back down where he lay between the railway tracks. Peering right and left through amber eyes, he wondered where his human had gone and why he'd been abandoned there in the dark. Had he done something wrong? Would someone come to help him?*

He sensed the train long before he heard it.

The metal tracks began to vibrate almost imperceptibly at first. The vibrations increased until they pulsed like an electric current through his body, making him quiver from top to tail.

Wriggling, he tried once more to raise himself, but still he couldn't move. The more he struggled, the more the pain shot through his lower body.

Cocking his head to one side, his finely tuned hearing picked up the rumbling of the approaching train as the tracks shivered and shook beneath him. Then the spotlights of the freight locomotive were looming towards him like the oncoming headlights of a car. An unstoppable machine, its destination was the massive goods and marshalling yard adjacent to New Spitalfields fruit and vegetable market in East London.

Still straining and trying to use his size and strength to overcome the pain that pinned him in the path of the monster, the big dog billowed clouds of steamy breath. But no matter how much he wrestled, he couldn't escape.

Whimpering, he turned his head quizzically to look up at the driver illuminated high in his cab – completely oblivious to what was about to happen as his chain of thirty-ton wagons sped closer and closer to where the creature lay.

The driver couldn't say later what it was that made him glance down on to the tracks at the last minute. Maybe it was the look in the dog's eyes, or could it have been a final, desperate bark?

Either way, there was nothing he could do but let out a small cry as he felt the train give a slight jolt before rattling on into the night.

1

*'All the darkness in the world cannot extinguish
the light of a single candle.'*

St Francis of Assisi

NOBODY CAN BE certain how the dog who was later designated 'Stray: E10' came to be on the railway tracks that bitter night of 9 January 2012. Few could fathom what kind of human being would abandon a five-month-old Anatolian Shepherd in a securely fenced-off area on a busy railway line with no means of escape. Those who found him thought he may have been clubbed around the head and face with a blunt instrument and thrown on to the line. Some reports claimed that he may have been tied to the tracks and speculated that the wheels of the train severed his bonds, allowing him to escape further injury.

Only one person knows the full story – the man with a foreign accent who was responsible for the defenceless animal that night. He was spotted briefly on the tracks by a railway operations manager minutes before the dog was found, but he scurried off into the darkness before any searching questions could be asked. Not surprisingly, he never came forward to claim the animal he'd left behind.

No matter what the precise circumstances of the events that led to the near-fatal mutilation of the handsome young dog, everyone agrees that it was an act of barbaric cruelty.

It could have been the work of a madman, or the result of a deal gone wrong. Perhaps the long-legged hound was no longer cute enough to make his breeder the £500-plus that Anatolian Shepherds frequently fetched. He might have been as large as a Labrador, but he was still only a puppy and puppies can be both demanding and expensive.

Nor does anyone know exactly what happened next. The driver who first reported hitting an animal on the line wasn't even initially sure it was a dog and he certainly didn't believe the creature could have survived the impact. Part of him must have hoped that its death had been quick and painless.

The first miracle, though, is that the dog wasn't killed outright. Somehow, as the goods train bore down upon him, he managed to flatten himself against the track-bed and avoid fatal injuries. Sadly, he was unable to escape the train altogether and the wheels almost severed his back left leg.

The second miracle is that – driven by an innate instinct to escape from danger – he somehow managed to lift his shattered body on to his uninjured legs and limp away, leaving a telltale trail of blood.

There can be no disputing that he would have been in acute pain as he pulled himself across to what he must have hoped was a place of safety, where he slumped between adjacent tracks. Little did he know that, in that busy rail corridor, with only narrow shingle banks on either side, he was still directly in the line of freight and passenger traffic.

No one can know how long after the first impact the abandoned Anatolian Shepherd lay there in the cold – without food or water, losing blood, sniffing at and occasionally licking his wounds. Further train drivers who spotted him near what is known locally as the Ruckholt Road Junction, on the edge of Hackney Marsh and Leyton, alerted staff working in the operations control room. Someone there then contacted the network's mobile operations manager, Nigel Morris, and asked him to investigate, but it was decided not to shut down the vital rail lifeline until there had been a direct sighting of the injured animal and confirmation that it was still alive.

Carrying a torch and letting himself into the secure area via a locked metal gate, Nigel began searching for a dog on the line. The area where it had been sighted was extremely busy that night, with a total of four lines carrying passenger trains to London's Stansted Airport and Cambridge, as well as freight trains to and from the goods yard.

Nigel was initially directed to the Temple Mills area,

where barking had been heard, but it turned out to be a guard dog patrolling a locked trading estate. He started making his way back down the track in the other direction when suddenly he came across a man walking along the line towards him in the dark. The heavy-set stranger had two huge dogs with him – an Alsatian and a Mastiff, both on short leashes. Nigel couldn't understand how the interloper had managed to get through multiple fences and tight security with two big dogs. He had a far more pressing concern, however: trains were still passing them, so he quickly used his radio to report a trespasser on the line and call for the trains to be stopped.

As Nigel drew closer to the stranger, he called out and asked him what he was doing there. The man, who was in his forties and around six feet tall with what sounded like an Eastern European accent, seemed completely unfazed. He claimed that he was looking for his dog. Strangely, though, he was walking away from where Nigel had been told an injured dog had been seen.

As Nigel's chief concern was to get the man off the track and to safety, he let him and his dogs out through the nearest access gate and quickly radioed that the trains could start running again. He called after the stranger to tell him that he'd keep looking for his dog, but was surprised when the man showed no interest and scurried off. Nigel watched him slope away into the darkness, then carried on searching along the track with his torch until eventually he spotted what he later described as a 'shadow between the rails'.

It was a dog, just lying there flat on its chest without moving. Nigel approached cautiously, although he assumed that it was dead and that he would have to deal with the body. When he got closer, however, he saw to his surprise that the animal was still alive, though its left rear leg and paw were covered in blood.

Nigel quickly realized that the dog was not only docile but too severely injured to attack him. He tried to shift it off the rails but ended up with blood all over his clothes and shoes; it was clear he wouldn't be able to manage on his own. He called his control room and asked them to contact the RSPCA and get them to send one of their officers to help him. Then he stayed near the injured dog and waited.

The RSPCA's uniformed welfare officer on duty in East London that winter's night was Siobhan Trinnaman, so it was she who received the call just after 7 p.m. to attend a 'dog on the line'. Having taken a note of the postcode – somewhere in E10 – she jumped into her Citroën Berlingo van with the distinctive RSPCA logo on the side and drove to the area, which lay in the shadow of the massive new Olympics site.

Nigel Morris met her on the street and unlocked an access gate which allowed them to pass through the secure fencing erected as part of the Olympics 'ring of steel'. Siobhan eventually found herself standing on the perilously narrow shingle strip at the edge of the busy line that transported people and produce across the country and beyond. As trains continued to trundle past, she picked her way over the uneven pebbly ground to where Nigel had discovered the dog. Shining the beam of her torch left and right she eventually found the animal lying between the tracks. She could see immediately that it was in a bad way and bleeding heavily. Standing a safe distance from where it lay, Siobhan played her torchlight along its body and noted that it was a male dog with serious injuries to its lower limbs. She was relieved to see him lift his head and look straight at her.

Then she heard something that made her gasp. Jumping back against a fence, she realized that another train was approaching.

Nigel quickly reassured her. 'It's okay,' he said. 'Watch. The dog knows what to do. The trains just ride over it. There's just enough room as long as it doesn't try to get up.'

The two of them pressed back and held their breath as a passenger train rattled towards the dog at a speed of around 45 m.p.h. Siobhan watched in amazement as the animal, ears flattened to his head, simply lay back down and let the train rumble over him. As soon as the final carriage had passed, he lifted his head again – ears pricked – and looked across at them to reassure himself that they were still there.

The minute she saw the pleading look in his eyes, Siobhan begged Nigel to get the line shut down as quickly as possible.

With so many urban foxes, stray dogs and cats crisscrossing Britain's busy train tracks every day, it is

Network Rail's policy not to shut down a line for an animal and no longer even to caution train drivers. They can, however, order a signaller to carry out what is known as a 'line blockage' if people or animals are considered to be in direct danger. Nigel radioed his control room and had the line temporarily closed for the second time that night so that he and Siobhan could cross safely to where the injured dog lay. As soon as they were promised that all trains had been stopped in both directions further up the tracks, they hurried to his side.

The first thing Siobhan noticed was that the top of the dog's head was noticeably swollen. In her five years as an RSPCA officer she had seen countless victims of abuse and cruelty, and experience told her he'd been hit on the head by something – most likely a blunt instrument. A train would have done far more damage. His leg and tail were badly mangled, and his tail especially was losing blood. She couldn't tell if he had any internal injuries but he didn't appear to be too tender inside when she examined him and she knew a trained vet would be able to establish exactly what was wrong.

In spite of his injuries, the dog seemed sweet-natured and not at all like so many she had had to deal with in her line of duty. A lot of animals as badly hurt as he was would have growled if she even came close and would almost certainly have tried to bite her; she carried a muzzle just in case. This gentle giant didn't seem to mind her touching him at all, though, and only whimpered a little when she did so.

Siobhan had the authority to order that an animal in distress or seriously injured could be put to sleep at the scene by a vet if she thought it was beyond help. However, because this dog didn't appear to be injured anywhere else and was, as she later said, so 'lovely and friendly', she made the decision there and then to try to save him.

With some difficulty, she and Nigel took one end of the dog each and managed to get him up on to three legs before carrying him a couple of hundred yards to where she'd parked her van. Apart from the odd whimper, he barely made a sound as they moved him and then lifted him into the back. As she wasn't qualified as a vet, Siobhan carried no pain relief, but she settled him on to bedding on his uninjured side and thanked the operations manager for his help.

Although Nigel Morris had been working for Network Rail for twelve years, that January night in 2012 was the first time he'd ever had to deal with an injured dog on the railway line. An animal lover, whose parents had two much-loved dogs back home in Trinidad, he said later that he would gladly have adopted this injured Anatolian Shepherd if his working life had allowed him to have a pet; there was just something about the dog that really struck him. He watched as Siobhan's van sped away and really hoped the poor creature would make it.

Siobhan drove as quickly as she could to the RSPCA's Harmsworth Memorial Animal Hospital in Holloway, North London. The hospital, which provides a twenty-four-hour, low-cost veterinary service for people on reduced incomes, was built in 1968 thanks to a donation from newspaper magnate Sir Harold Harmsworth, 1st Viscount Rothermere. Student vets train here and staff treat more than nine thousand animals every year – including many stray and injured dogs.

The young dog who'd been found on the railway tracks cried out a couple of times during the twenty-five-minute journey to Harmsworth, especially whenever his tail or leg touched the side of the van, but apart from that he was surprisingly stoical. When Siobhan eventually arrived, her clothes still covered in his blood, she was assisted by two of the vet nurses who helped her lift him on to a trolley and wheeled him inside.

Stan McCaskie, the hospital's clinical director and the senior vet on duty that night, saw to the dog immediately in the prep room, examining his wounds and doing all he could to stem the bleeding.

'I'll never forget seeing this big dog wheeled towards me on the trolley, half sitting up and looking all around him,' he said later. 'He seemed most amenable and almost relaxed. When I was told he'd been hit by a train I couldn't believe it. I prayed that he still had both his back legs, which are the ones that are usually lost. Fortunately, he had one good leg left, but the other was stripped of all its skin and crushed flat from above the ankle right down to the end of his paw.'

Stan, who first came to England on a scholarship from Barbados in 1989 to study to be a vet and has been at

Harmsworth for twenty-four years, knew that the important thing was to stabilize the dog after the shock of his experience. He placed him on a drip to rehydrate him, gave him some painkillers and antibiotics, and then cleaned and dressed his wounds, which included an impact injury to his lip that required stitching and a contusion or bruise to his head. His tail was almost completely severed and Stan knew he would lose it along with his rear leg, but after such a trauma the first thing to do was to make sure he survived the next few days. This was critical, otherwise they might well lose him under the anaesthetic.

The staff laid the dog on a duvet in a warm, quiet, walk-in kennel and the vet nurses on duty were asked to monitor him throughout the night. For a while it was touch and go whether he'd make it at all, and several who saw him there fully expected him not to.

Stan McCaskie went back to his night shift and some surgery on a wounded cat, and that was the last he saw of the injured dog. 'So often we have cases come in and we treat them and then never see or hear of them again,' he said. 'I didn't have any follow-up with the Anatolian Shepherd, but I never forgot him. He had such a lovely way about him.'

Siobhan Trinnaman felt the same. When she left the dog she'd officially listed in the record books as 'Stray: E10' in the care of the hospital that night, she knew there was a chance that he might not survive. The thought saddened her. 'He really stuck in my mind, and not just because of where and how he was found,' she remembered later. 'There was a look in his eyes that made me think about him long afterwards.'

Even those at Harmsworth who were accustomed to animal cruelty – an estimated 15 per cent of their cases are caused by violence or neglect – were shocked by what had happened to their newest patient. Veterinary staff who'd previously rescued animals involved in dogfights, or that had been stabbed or beaten until their bones were broken, did all they could to keep this one alive too. It was clear that he'd been hit over the head and the general feeling was that he must have been knocked unconscious or maybe even tied somehow so that he couldn't get out of the path of the train. It was so sad to see a beautiful young animal like that in such a terrible state and 'Stray: E10' won the hearts of everyone who saw him, not least because, although he was so poorly and had been sedated, he still looked up hopefully every time anyone came near.

Michelle Hurley was one of the first to see the wounded animal soon after he'd been settled into his kennel on that first night. She volunteered for a charity based in North London called All Dogs Matter and she visited Harmsworth and other shelters two or three times a week. Relying largely on volunteers, All Dogs Matter rescues some 250–300 dogs a year and rehomes them to foster carers all over the country, and they take in as many from Harmsworth as they can. As part of her job helping find homes for strays, Michelle frequently takes photographs of the animals, which she then posts on various rescue websites. Whenever there's a success story with a rescue animal the charity uses such 'before and after' images to highlight animal cruelty – but they are often distressing pictures to take. She took some shots of the injured Anatolian while he still had his mangled leg and was looking extremely sorry for himself.

The injured dog survived his first night at the hospital and then the next, and those caring for him began to feel more hopeful. No owner came forward to claim him or to report a dog of his description missing; nor was he microchipped, which was unusual for such an expensive and relatively rare breed. Staff believed this pointed more and more towards an act of deliberate cruelty.

Over the next few days a second RSPCA vet, Fiona Buchan, met with her colleagues to discuss what to do with their patient. Although he was such a kind and gentle dog, they knew he was going to grow into a massive animal and they wondered how such a big dog would cope with three legs. They did debate whether it might be kinder to put him to sleep at that point. If he had lost a front leg, they almost certainly would have done so, but in the end they decided to give him a chance.

Once the shock of being hit by the train had worn off, the injured dog was in a lot of pain from his injuries, which were so severe the vets didn't even X-ray them. There was no point – the leg and tail were crushed to a red pulp and couldn't be saved.

Once she'd assessed that he had stabilized enough for major surgery, Fiona anaesthetized him and removed his tail almost to the base of the spine and his leg close to the hip. If she'd waited any longer, infection might have set in. As is the policy of the hospital in the case of strays, she also neutered him. Fiona said later, 'I just hoped then that the right home could be found for him. I knew he wouldn't be an easy dog to place, but, strangely, what had happened to him and the fact that he had three legs probably made him more appealing and gave him a better chance of standing out from the crowd.' In what she described as an 'often thankless job', she said that this canine patient stayed in her mind long after she had operated on him: 'There was something about him that made him worth going the extra mile.'

No one knew the big dog's name, but one by one the staff fell for the animal they described as a 'cuddly bear'. Despite the cruelty inflicted on him, their new patient constantly craved human affection. As before, almost as soon as he came round from the anaesthetic he tried to get up to greet anyone who approached him. Those who'd witnessed dogs beaten within an inch of their lives who still wagged their tails when they saw a human agreed that the forgiving Anatolian Shepherd with just a postcode for an epithet needed a proper name. 'Stray: E10' seemed too clinical and 'Tripod' (the other name most commonly used by the RSPCA for three-legged dogs) didn't do him justice.

Then a man named Alex who worked with Michelle at All Dogs Matter came up with the name 'Haatchi' and everyone agreed that it was perfect. The name stuck. It was a variation of Hachi, which was the nickname of a pure-bred Japanese Akita dog called Hachikō in the 1920s who was so devoted to his master that he waited every night at the train station for him to return home from work. (The name Hachikō means 'faithful dog number 8' – he was eighth pup in the litter – and also 'a prince'.) Then one day in May 1925 Hachi's master, Professor Hidesaburo Ueno, suffered a cerebral haemorrhage at the University of Tokyo where he worked and he never came home. For the next ten years, until his own death, Hachi arrived at the station at precisely the hour of his master's evening train and waited for him in vain. Commuters who saw him night after night soon befriended him and gave him food and treats as news of his unstinting loyalty spread. Articles were published about him and Hachi became a sensation. He was cited to schoolchildren as the finest example of the fidelity they should exhibit both to their parents and to their emperor, and Hachi soon became a source of national pride.

A bronze statue created by a famous artist was erected in his honour at the station – in his presence – and although it later had to be melted down and recycled for the war effort, the son of the original artist later created a replica. The monument became a popular rendezvous site at the station; it is still known today as 'the Hachikō entrance' and the expression 'Meet you at Hachikō' would still be understood by most Tokyo-dwellers. The exact spot where he waited is also marked with bronze pawprints.

When Hachi eventually died in March 1935 – still patiently waiting for his master – his body was stuffed and mounted for display in the National Museum of Nature and Science in Tokyo; thousands queued to see him. Almost eighty years on, the museum shop still sells a model of him. Every year a service of remembrance is held at the station where Hachi waited and dog lovers from around the world attend in his memory. And in 1959, a previously undiscovered recording of Hachi barking was played on national Japanese radio for the first time, as millions tuned in.

The heart-warming story was eventually made into a film in Japan in 1987 and then in 2009 into a globally released movie set in America and starring Richard Gere, entitled *Hachi: A Dog's Tale*. Hachi has also been the subject of numerous children's books.

The young Anatolian Shepherd given the garbled variation of his name eighty years later and on another continent had only one link with the faithful Akita – a railway line. But he certainly seemed to share the loyal spirit of his noble namesake and endeared himself similarly to everyone who met him.

Even though he now had a name, Haatchi was far from saved. Everyone knew that, if he made it, he'd face a lot of expensive health problems that would only make it even harder to find him a suitable home. Any dog that has lost a leg to become what's known as a 'tripod' – or 'tri-pawed' – needs time and space to acclimatize to his new shape, gait and centre of gravity. There is a sudden loss of balance and stability, especially on uneven or slippery surfaces. As he tried to adapt to the transition, Haatchi fell over a lot and his frequent falls threatened to destabilize the healing stumps of his amputated leg and tail.

With one leg missing, his remaining back limb slowly became far more load-bearing and – as with all tripods – he began to reposition it to a more central point for support. He also started to turn out his paw for improved traction. All this would inevitably lead to arthritis and other problems in his right hip, knee and paw-pad.

As he gradually found his footing, though, Haatchi was eager to move out of his cage. He desperately needed a larger space than his confined quarters and was becoming stressed, whining constantly. Harmsworth Hospital needed him to be moved too. Their wards were so full that some animals had to be kept in cages in the corridors and the walk-in kennel was needed for other, now more urgent, cases.

Haatchi had arrived at that hospital as little more than a confused puppy, but in a matter of weeks he'd been forced to grow up very fast. He'd been through the worst experience of his life but had somehow emerged from it all the stronger. Although he was still recovering from his injuries, he'd done well enough to be considered for temporary fostering until he could be found a permanent home.

Hospital staff asked the team at All Dogs Matter if they could help. While a place was being sought for him,

RSPCA inspector Siobhan went to visit the dog she'd rescued for what she assumed was the last time.

'He was still so sweet,' she said. 'There was just a calmness and goodness about him that kept him at the forefront of my mind.' As she bade him farewell she knew that whatever happened to him next would be in other people's hands.

All Dogs Matter – whose chairman is the actor Peter Egan of *Ever Decreasing Circles* fame – has a huge network of foster carers all over the country and the organization's general manager Ira Moss became the next link in the human chain of kindness that would eventually lead Haatchi to what those in animal welfare refer to as his 'forever' home.

The charity had dealt with several dogs like Haatchi before, but Ira was especially concerned about the double indemnity of this one's injuries and the difficulties of placing his particular breed, which was developing an unfortunate reputation as being dangerous and aggressive.

Anatolian Shepherds, which are in part descended from Mastiffs, are also known as Turkish Shepherd Guard Dogs because of their success in protecting large flocks of sheep from predators in the harsh terrain of the central Anatolian region of Turkey. Watchful and possessive, this rugged breed dates back some six thousand years and boasts a broad, masked head and a short, dense coat for coping with extremes of hot and cold. They are gifted with superior sight and hearing, are powerful enough to take down wolves or even mountain lions and are sometimes known as 'lion hunters'. Full-grown Anatolians can reach heights of three feet, and these barrel-chested animals can weigh up to ten stone, yet they are known for their speed, endurance and stamina. Active, hard-working and intensely loyal, they come from what is known as a 'guardian' breed, which means that they will defend their 'flock' and fight predators to the death if they have to. Sadly, sometimes those predators can be seen as other dogs, or even humans.

One woman out walking her dog in Somerset in 2011 was badly mauled by three Anatolian Shepherds that had escaped from their home. They also killed her dog. At the ensuing court case the judge – who fined the owner £10,000 – declared that these kinds of dogs were 'not appropriate to be kept in England'. The attack made news headlines and threatened to brand the entire breed as dangerous.

Ira Moss knew that most rescued Anatolians in London tended to come from the Tottenham and Palmers Green areas, which have large Turkish and Kurdish communities. Some are used for dog-fighting, but others are bought for patriotic reasons and then become the victims of neglect or ignorance. They may start off as cute, fluffy puppies but they grow quickly and are bred to protect – even to the death – so they require early socialization with other dogs and humans. As with all large breeds, they need a lot of space, plenty of exercise, and a firm, confident handler who understands not only canine instinct but also the vigilant nature of the breed and can train them appropriately before they become too powerful to handle.

Inexperienced owners think that because these animals usually live permanently outdoors in their native land they can be left outside in the UK, even during the bitter winter months, which isn't always viable. Although their thick coats may be suited to extremes of climate, Anatolian Shepherd dogs left alone in gardens or yards will often bark incessantly, try to escape, or cause damage, which soon annoys their owners even though they themselves are usually the ones at fault.

When Ira was asked about finding a foster home for Haatchi, she initially contacted one of the charities specializing in Anatolian Shepherds, but their books were full and they couldn't take him in, so she approached one of the charity's regular foster carers instead. Lorraine Coyle, a dog-walker and minder from Hendon in North London, was told that the animal who needed her help might have been tied to a railway track and that he was still recovering from major surgery, and her heart went out to him. 'That poor dog must have had a terrible time,' she said, 'firstly because of what happened to him and then to wake up without a leg and tail and find that he'd been castrated by the RSPCA as well. Life was entirely different to how he remembered it.'

Lorraine was happy to take Haatchi in until he could be found a permanent home, so the handover was arranged and a volunteer from All Dogs Matter delivered him to her house. She had successfully fostered many times before, but it was soon apparent to her that this wouldn't be a normal case.

Although Haatchi was 'incredibly passive' and got along very well with her twelve-year-old Boxer, Bobby, he was still extremely traumatized. He was young and had a lot of energy, so he kept trying to run around, but he repeatedly fell and banged his stumps on the floor. They'd been stitched up, but his leg wound was still partially open and looked dreadful. 'Put it this way,' Lorraine explained, 'I have never been able to look at a leg of lamb since.'

A distressed Haatchi stayed with her for only one night. He spent it crashing around, banging himself and crying out each time, until she couldn't take any more. After a sleepless few hours, she could tell that he wasn't happy and she worried that he had no quality of life. She was also very concerned about his raw wounds and believed he needed ongoing veterinary attention. She rang the team at All Dogs Matter early the following morning and told them he needed to go back to Harmsworth Hospital.

Lorraine knew there was a risk that Haatchi might be put to sleep if he couldn't be found a suitable home, but there was also a moment when she wondered if that might even be the kinder option for him. Nevertheless, she told All Dogs Matter that once his wounds were fully healed, she'd gladly take him back. If the alternative was Haatchi being euthanized, then she was definitely prepared to try again.

As she never heard another word about the unhappy

three-legged dog who had spent a night in her home, Lorraine enquired about him a few weeks later and was told the charity had no further trace of him. Upset, she assumed that the poor animal must have been put to sleep. 'That was the last thing I wanted for him,' she said, 'but I don't honestly know what else I could have done.'

Although the RSPCA, Dogs Trust and other animal charities do all they can to save the almost 120,000 stray dogs abandoned every year in Britain – which amounts to 325 every day – an untold number of rescue animals (including cats and others) have to be put down because they're too badly injured, too sick, or simply cannot be found suitable homes. Of that overall figure, the Dogs Trust estimates that almost nine thousand dogs were put to sleep in 2012 alone – which equates to more than one dog every hour killed by lethal injection, usually with extreme reluctance by staff.

Each year the Trust commissions a survey of all UK local authorities (who took over responsibility for stray dogs from the police in 2008) to ascertain Britain's stray-dog problem. A research company asks how many dogs were seized by or handed in to council pounds, and then finds out how many were returned to their owners, rehomed or put to sleep.

In 2012, the survey found that 118,932 stray and abandoned dogs had been handled by 327 local authorities across the UK over the previous twelve months. Only 15 per cent of these dogs were brought in by the general public; the rest were seized by wardens and then placed in one of the few council pounds (the several hundred police kennels, most of them located at the back of police stations, were closed down under the 2008 legislation). If the council pounds are full, then the dogs are contracted out to commercial kennels at a cost to the taxpayer and the clock starts ticking.

The staff working at the numerous charitable rehoming centres up and down the country take in as many as they can too, but funding for animal charities has plummeted during the recession and they've also been inundated with extra unwanted pets as owners have dumped animals they can no longer afford to keep. A change in the policy of many local authorities has meant the banning of dogs from rented accommodation – even for existing tenants with pets – and that has only added to the influx.

Of all the dogs taken in by local authorities in 2012, 47 per cent were reunited with their owners, 9 per cent were rehomed, 24 per cent were passed on to welfare organizations or dog kennels, and 7 per cent were put to sleep – amounting to 8,903 animals. The remainder were either found dead or dying, or were taken in by those who first found them.

Although the overall figure of abandoned dogs discovered by the Dogs Trust represents a slight decrease from the previous year, the survey found that of the animals listed a significant percentage (23 per cent) were those breeds known as 'status dogs', such as Staffordshire Bull Terriers, Rottweilers, Akitas or larger crossbreeds. These dogs are perceived to be tougher looking, a factor which is deemed to improve their owner's social status. Used by youths and gangs as weapons of intimidation in streets and parks, they are often encouraged to display aggressive behaviour and are entered into illegal dogfights for money. Many animals suffer torture, neglect and violence at the hands of their owners – some of which is designed to make them even more aggressive. Indiscriminate breeding of such dogs to earn tax-free income only adds to the problem, and animal charities have reported an alarming rise in reports of dogfights and puppy farms specializing in the status breeds.

Some charities have claimed that they are facing a 'tidal wave' of cruelty cases that is threatening to overwhelm them. Cases have also flooded in from European countries such as some of the former Eastern Bloc nations where the culture towards animal welfare is often less enlightened than it is in the UK.

The RSPCA's animal cruelty report for 2012 showed that its four hundred inspectors submitted 2,093 cases and 3,181 individuals to its Prosecutions Department, resulting in 4,168 convictions in the courts. This represented a 34 per cent rise on the previous year and featured some of the worst cases ever seen.

In light of this fresh influx, Britain's largest animal welfare charity changed its policy in 2010 so that it no longer takes in animals that are merely 'unwanted'. The RSPCA was, however, able to find the right pet for more than fifty-five thousand families and individuals who went to its shelters or visited its websites online in 2012.

That happy ending hadn't happened yet for Haatchi, though, and after his brief experience of foster care he was returned to Harmsworth Hospital. The future for any dog returned from fostering is increasingly bleak, as staff fear the animal might be impossible to place – especially if it has serious and pre-existing medical problems that are likely to be ongoing, uninsurable and costly, just as Haatchi did.

Most people would agree that the vets and nursing staff who work for the RSPCA do an amazing job in the face of an onslaught of abandoned or mistreated animals, but there is only so much they can do – especially with so many new strays brought into their hard-pressed shelters every day. Rescue charities claim they've known of numerous instances where vets have operated on animals to save their lives and then kept them for far longer than they were meant to, only to have to place them on the dreaded PTS (Put to Sleep) list a few weeks later because more abuse cases were coming in than they could possibly handle.

Haatchi, it seemed, had survived being hit by a train only to face the possibility of a very different kind of death.

Fortunately for him and others like him, there is an untold number of anonymous volunteers who do what they can to save PTS animals on Death Row. Known as 'pound pullers', these vets, veterinary nurses, volunteers and kennel staff regularly take photographs of the dogs most at risk in the hope that they will be 'pulled' from the dog pound before it is too late. They post their pictures on a series of online registers, telephone anyone they can think of who might be able to help, or wait for one of the many hundreds of charities throughout the UK with a 'No Kill' policy to take pity on the condemned animal.

Michelle Hurley from All Dogs Matter still had her photos of Haatchi on her mobile phone and it was she who now posted them on a website named Rescue Helpers Unite. This non-profit organization, formed of unpaid volunteers from around the country, has a huge database of fosterers, home-checkers and transporters, and has helped more than fourteen thousand animals since it was started in 2007.

Anatolian Shepherds are relatively rare in the rescue world, so it was hoped that, in spite of his many problems, Haatchi would be spotted by a kind stranger and saved.

Suzanne Syers works full-time as a chiropodist but her childhood love of German Shepherds spurred her to set up the UK German Shepherd Rescue charity in 2010. She has seven rescue Shepherds of her own and had been fostering for other charities for years when she decided to go it alone and set up her own. It is now the second largest breed-specific charity in the UK. Run from her home in Warrington, in Cheshire, the UKGSR under Suzanne and her team has saved more than five hundred German Shepherds since it began and – as its reputation grows – 'pound pullers' know to contact her directly if they have any Shepherds at risk.

UKGSR tends to go for the animals in the most urgent need. By law all strays that haven't been injured or are not unwell are taken to council kennels and held for seven days. From the eighth day, they're at risk of being put to sleep if they can't be rehomed, so their details are posted on as many rescue forums as possible. Status dogs like Staffordshire Bull Terriers and crossbreeds bear the brunt of current trends and their troubled faces fill the websites, sparking what some have described as a 'Staffie holocaust'. Then there are the ones like Haatchi, who have been rescued and treated by the RSPCA and have usually been in care for much longer than the unwanted status dogs. Once they get better, the clock starts ticking for them too.

Suzanne Syers spends most mornings trawling through the rescue sites looking for Shepherds and trying to assess how desperate their need is. One morning in January 2012 she was sitting at her computer when she clicked on the photo of Haatchi on the Rescue Helpers Unite forum. 'I took one look at his face and that was it!' she recalled.

Even though Haatchi wasn't a German Shepherd, he was of the Shepherd breed and that endeared him to Suzanne enough to persuade her to step in and help him. In truth, she thinks she would have saved him anyway. The intense look in his eyes was compelling.

All the listing stated was that Haatchi had been hit by a train and had a leg removed. She knew no more than that, and she didn't want to know. It doesn't matter to UKGSR what has happened in a dog's past; they try to focus only on its future. Suzanne knew that the trouble with a dog like Haatchi was that other people would see him and automatically think 'vet bills'. They would also be afraid of how much it would cost to feed him. She wasn't that surprised that no one had yet come forward to save him.

She rang Harmsworth Hospital and spoke to a veterinary nurse, who admitted she was worried that Haatchi was on borrowed time and might be put to sleep the following week. That was on a Sunday, so Suzanne promised her they'd take him straight away.

It was Haatchi's lucky day. Suzanne Syers was probably his last chance.

Keen to act quickly, she rang the UKGSR London and South East coordinator Tracey Harris, a veteran fundraiser and charity worker, at her home in Berkshire to see if she could find someone to collect Haatchi and take him to safety as soon as possible. Tracey, who also runs a charity called A Better Life which rescues dogs from Romania, made further enquiries and was told that not only had Haatchi been hit by a train, but he might have been tied to the tracks. She was shocked – she simply couldn't imagine someone doing such a thing, but she knew the RSPCA don't make up those kinds of stories.

She hit the phones straight away to see where they could place him. Tracey knew the priority was to get him out of Harmsworth as quickly as possible. She believed that whoever had posted his photo was probably clutching at straws: the RSPCA had rescued Haatchi from the railway line and fought to save his life, so any decision to put him to sleep would not be taken lightly, but sometimes they have to make tough calls in order to be able to save other animals.

While she was looking for a suitable foster home and posting Haatchi's photo on Facebook, Tracey contacted one of her volunteers, Nicola Collinson, who lives near Stansted in Essex, and it was agreed that she or one of their other recruits would take him in until a suitable placing could be found. Suzanne asked her to go as quickly as she could to Harmsworth Hospital, which Nicola knew of, as it is where the award-winning BBC television series *Animal Hospital* was filmed – a programme she'd loved.

This was Nicola's first job for UKGSR and she didn't really know what to expect. When she was told she'd be collecting an Anatolian Shepherd she had no idea what that was exactly, or how big. She owned a six-month-old German Shepherd called Vinnie so she assumed this dog would be a similar size.

Nicola gave up her Sunday and jumped into her Volkswagen Golf to drive to Holloway as quickly as she could. When she got there she found that the hospital was in a rough area and didn't look at all welcoming from the outside. She thought it was like Fort Knox, with high security all around; it certainly seemed nothing like she'd seen on the TV show.

All the doors were locked, so she rang the bell and hoped for the best. She realized that she had no paperwork with her and was worried that the staff might not even allow her to take the dog away. Fortunately, the lady who let her in seemed to be expecting her.

Nicola was asked to sit in a waiting area and was still wondering what to expect when a door opened and in lolloped a huge dog with a leg missing and just a stump of a tail. One look at that face and Nicola decided that if they couldn't find Haatchi a foster home, then she would definitely take him herself.

'He limped across to me all wobbly on three legs and placed his big head on my lap,' she recalled. 'Then he looked up at me with those big brown and yellow eyes and I melted. I laughed and told him, "Blimey, you're enormous! How am I going to get you in my car?"'

The member of staff who had let Nicola into the hospital helped her lift him into her Golf, where Haatchi was as good as gold. He sat on a soft bed in the back and just looked out of the window as if this was the most natural thing in the world.

Nicola checked her phone for messages and found one from Tracey Harris asking her to take Haatchi to South Mimms motorway services on the M25 in Hertfordshire. She had found someone who would foster him and Nicola was to drive to a far corner of the car park and wait for a Land Rover. After falling for the big bear in the back of her car, a part of her was a little disappointed.

Ross McCarthy and James Hearle run a company called Dogs and Kisses in Oxfordshire. James trained in agriculture and worked in animal welfare until he set up the top-notch doggy daycare/foster home; his partner Ross is a respected animal behaviourist and both are experts in dog and cat behaviour. The two men had seen Haatchi's photo as an emergency case on Facebook and immediately offered to foster him. They already had eleven dogs of their own, including several Great Danes, and Tracey knew that with their experience and background they'd be ideal for a so-called 'problem' dog.

Once they were given the green light, Ross and James also dropped what they were doing and hurried to the motorway services to meet Haatchi for the first time.

Meanwhile, Nicola was driving towards them from the opposite direction. Hoping it would keep him calm, she chatted to Haatchi all the way across London as he sat in the back. When they reached South Mimms, she thought she'd better let him relieve himself, so she opened the back door and helped him out.

That's when she realized she'd never be able to get him back in again on her own. So the two of them sat together beside her car as she carried on chatting, while he sniffed at the ground and occasionally tilted his head at her as if he was listening to her every word.

Eventually, a Land Rover pulled up next to them and Ross and James stepped out. All three of them started laughing, because they said it felt as if they were drug dealers doing 'something dodgy' in the corner of a car park. The two men immediately liked the look of Haatchi and commented on what 'a lovely big bear' he was. They all watched then as – without fuss or fear – he limped over to where they were waiting and allowed them to lift him into the back of their vehicle. Ross was struck by how calm and easy he was to deal with. It was as if he knew they were saving him.

Less than twenty-four hours after his face had been plastered over computer screens around the UK and Suzanne Syers had spotted it, Haatchi was safe.

'There's something about Haatchi that's hard to explain,' Suzanne said later. 'He is massively special and has definitely been in this life before. He has such an air about him, and takes everything in his three-legged stride. Nothing fazes him. It's as if he knows what he is here on this earth to do and he is intent on just getting on and doing that job as well as he can.'

Nobody, not even Haatchi, could have predicted how important a job he had ahead of him – especially for one little boy.

For both of them, a brand-new life was about to begin.

2

OWEN HOWKINS WAS a funny, smart and courageous little boy – although few beyond his immediate family realized it.

One of the reasons his sweet nature was rarely enjoyed by others was that the six-year-old boy with a rare muscular condition curled in on himself physically almost every time he was taken out of his home in his wheelchair.

'People are staring at me!' he'd complain to the large and loving extended family that has always surrounded and supported him. Whenever he said things like that he would break their hearts anew.

Owen was born on 25 August 2005 in a hospital in Dundee. His dad, Will, and mum, Kim, were both in the armed forces and based at RAF Leuchars nearby. They'd met on a training course in October 2002 when Kim was nineteen and Will was twenty-four and were married near her parents' home in Devon on a cold January day two years later. They both remember it as a very happy event.

Will, a senior aircraftsman with a specialization in propulsion, had already served in Kosovo and Croatia when the couple met and he was due to be sent on his first tour of Iraq. Kim, a fellow aircraftswoman and weapons technician, was soon to be deployed similarly. In spite of their busy and sometimes dangerous lives, the news of Owen's impending arrival was a cause for great celebration – he would be a first grandchild for both Will's and Kim's parents, who all lived in southern England. Almost as soon as Kim found out she was pregnant, the couple made plans to move back home for extra support from both families. They dearly wanted a child, but with both of them working in jobs that could send them over-seas for months at a time, they knew they'd almost certainly need some help.

Owen's birth went normally and as far as everyone was concerned he was a perfect baby. The only thing Kim spotted was that the top of one of his ears had curled in a little – a detail that most people wouldn't even have noticed. (Later on, the couple found out that this was a characteristic of the syndrome with which he would eventually be diagnosed.)

Will took to fatherhood instantly and became hands on. Kim says that from the word go her husband was a brilliant dad and describes him as a 'very modern man' whom she couldn't fault. When she suffered from post-natal depression, Will immediately stepped in to help, getting up most nights to feed their son and change his nappy. Then when she went back to work when Owen was four months old they shared his care whenever he wasn't at nursery. About six months after Owen was born Will and Kim were posted to RAF Odiham in Hampshire.

The new parents coped well at first, not least because their baby slept ten hours straight every night, plus naps. They assumed they were just lucky. With the help of Kim's parents, Sara and Hugh Knott, and Will's mum and dad, Bill and Joan Howkins, they formed a close-knit and cohesive family.

All the early photographs of Owen show a happy, plump baby. His health visitor assured his parents that he was completely normal, but as the months passed they began to wonder if he was thriving as well as he should for his age. He seemed to pick up every cold, and he was a hot and sweaty child. Before long he started coughing frequently and then being sick at night. They tried not to worry.

In 2006, Will was deployed to Iraq and Kim stayed at home to juggle the stresses of motherhood with her demanding job as an armourer. Fortunately, she, Will and Owen had always been surrounded by an amazingly supportive network of families and friends and she relied on them for help with childcare whenever she was working.

By the time Owen was eighteen months old, though, it was clear he wasn't developing completely normally. Both sets of grandparents began to notice that he seemed to be a late starter and was crawling 'like a tortoise', it was so laborious. His cousin Molly was a year younger but Owen looked to be the baby next to her. Friends and family began to worry, and they weren't the only ones.

Will and Kim had noticed that their son wasn't crawling so much as dragging himself along. He was also losing his baby fat too quickly and not going to the toilet normally. They took him to the doctor, who examined him and felt tight muscles in his tummy, which he assumed meant the baby was constipated. He gave him some medicine, but it didn't work and Owen continued to lose weight.

In March 2007, Kim was sent to Qatar for four months and Will was left home alone to look after his son, as well as working full-time. Those weren't easy days.

Will's parents had Owen stay with them for a weekend to give him a break, but when he went to collect him they asked him to sit down and hear them out. Although they were eager not to be seen as interfering grandparents, they nevertheless told Will that they thought he should take his son to see a specialist. Having had him with them for a few days, they were alarmed to see how slow his crawling was and also noticed that his movements were stiff and robotic. He didn't seem able to bend his knees.

Bill Howkins, a retired fire station commander turned fire safety consultant, found it very hard to broach the subject. Owen called Bill his 'Nee-Nah' Granddad because of the noise a fire engine makes and Bill loved the boy dearly. He and his wife, Joan, who had trained as a nurse, didn't want to speak out of turn, but almost from the start they had had a growing sense of dread that there might be something seriously wrong with their grandson. In their minds they feared everything from autism to leukaemia, and Joan thought he might also be partially blind. They didn't know if the problem was physical or mental, as Owen would become unreasonably upset if they skipped a verse in one of his favourite nursery rhymes or moved one of his toys out of the perfect alignment he'd created. Instead of being a bouncing, healthy baby, he was poorly and pale and had a nasty cough that wouldn't go away. They were the first to admit that Will was a 'natural' father and they weren't critical of him in any way, but they also felt it was time to act and assured him they only wanted to help.

Around the same time, Kim's parents also expressed their concerns. They had recently returned from a two-week holiday in Portugal with Owen. While they were away with him, they noticed that he cried a lot and was sweating constantly. When Sara gave him a bath she saw how unusually well-defined his muscles were – with bulging biceps and abs that she described as 'like a miniature body-builder'. It wasn't normal, and she knew he should have been walking by then too. They did all they could to encourage Owen to take his first few steps in the hope that he could surprise Will and Kim when they met them at the airport, but he just couldn't manage it.

The opinions of his parents and parents-in-law

mattered deeply to Will; he'd always said that whatever advice they had about bringing up children, he and Kim would at least listen. But although secretly he was beginning to have his own worries about his son's late development, nothing prepared him for what they were suggesting, and their fears upset him. 'He was our first and only child, so to Kim and me, Owen was still perfect,' he said. 'I guess we were both in denial.'

Will sat on what his parents had told him for a week. He tried to reassure himself there was nothing wrong, but in the back of his mind he noticed more and more things Owen was unable to do, and he started to become frightened of the outcome. Most noticeably, Owen couldn't walk unaided at all; he was using little plastic golf clubs as a way of supporting himself. Will took them away from him to try to get him to walk normally, but he couldn't do it.

With Kim still away working on the other side of the world, Will asked the health visitor to assess their son again. She put Owen through a series of tests that could be checked off against a growth chart but eventually she referred him to the Basingstoke and North Hampshire Hospital.

Kim was allowed to make only one phone call home a week for twenty minutes' duration, so on her next call Will used what little time they had to try to explain what was happening. She was as worried as he was; in many ways it was worse for her because she was so far away. She didn't admit it to Will until later, but she had already secretly begun to fear that Owen might be autistic. She had noticed how methodical he was about the tiniest details, and how he liked to line everything up, even his grapes before eating them. He was also very quick mentally and was good at puzzles and tests.

As the weeks and months went by, Owen's body began to tighten and his face became pinched to the point that people started staring at him. His family dressed him in a T-shirt whenever they took him swimming so that nobody would notice how different his body looked from those of the other children. His voice was higher-pitched than normal too, and it was becoming more and more apparent that something wasn't right.

His doctors arranged a succession of urgent tests as they tried to figure out what was wrong. They first mentioned the possibility of something called Thomsen's disease, or congenital myotonia, where the muscles have an exaggerated response and fail to release each time they contract, resulting in the kind of cramping they were seeing in Owen. In many such cases, warming the muscles helps the spasms created by the condition and patients often need no further treatment; however, that didn't work for Owen. Baffled, his medical team eventually referred the family to the Wessex Clinical Genetics Service at Southampton General Hospital, which works closely with geneticists based at Southampton University.

With Kim still away and 'worried out of her mind', Bill and Joan Howkins accompanied their son and grandson to the first major clinical meeting to lend moral support.

They realized something was seriously wrong the minute they walked into the room and found themselves faced with six doctors. They knew that this wasn't normal in the NHS, and the sight of all those grave-faced experts waiting for them only increased their anxieties even further.

Dr Neil Thomas, the head of department, wrote something down on a piece of paper and told them this was what he thought Owen might have. The words he wrote were 'Schwartz-Jampel syndrome'. It was the first the family had ever heard of it.

Dr Thomas has seen more than five thousand patients in his career as consultant paediatric neurologist specializing in neuromuscular disease, but he had never personally come across a case of Schwartz-Jampel syndrome before. Nor had any of his colleagues. The condition was first identified as recently as 1962, and the doctor believed that Owen's was the first case of its kind known in the UK; he told them that fewer than a hundred cases had ever been reported worldwide.

He explained that the toddler was showing signs of what is known as a myotonic condition, in which muscles fail to relax after they contract. He said it was a bit like someone shaking your hand and then not being able to let go. Because of the continual contraction, the muscles become increasingly stiff and tight, putting constant pressure on the skeleton. This applied pressure eventually prevents the bones from growing naturally and creates certain distinctive characteristics of the syndrome, including reduced stature and the 'pigeon breast' that can interfere with the up-and-down movement of the ribcage in breathing. Those affected also develop a specific look as their facial muscles tighten, scrunching their features, squeezing shut their eyes and pursing their lips. A curled-in ear can be another early indicator. Many have affected eyesight, special dental needs and a higher than normal pitch to their voice.

The family was told that there are two main types of the syndrome, of which 1B is much the worse and usually manifests itself at birth. In those cases patients normally live only until their mid-teens. Dr Thomas explained that because Owen had not shown symptoms until eighteen months of age, he was almost certain to have type 1A, which meant he should be able to lead a relatively full life.

The difficulty is that the syndrome affects people in different ways, so there is no blueprint or classic case by which new patients can be gauged. As with others with the syndrome, Owen was found to have a mutation in what is known as the 'perlecan' gene, but each case depends on where the mutation in the gene is and what it does to that gene.

At the moment around thirty people in the world – as far afield as Nepal, Saudi Arabia, the United States and Europe – are known to be living with Schwartz-Jampel syndrome, many of whom were in their teens or older before they were finally and formally diagnosed. Almost all of them have to take powerful muscle-relaxants just to be able to function.

The news that Owen had the rare syndrome was so shocking to Will and his parents that they could barely take it all in. Listening to what the doctors were telling them was very hard, and extremely emotional. There were far more questions than answers at this first meeting. Primarily, the family wanted to know how the syndrome was likely to affect Owen and what his long-term prognosis was likely to be.

They were told he would almost certainly need frequent physiotherapy to help ease the pressure of his contracted muscles on his skeleton. He might also have to wear splints to stretch his leg muscles, and he could face a series of operations as he grew up. There was a chance that he would spend his later life confined to a wheelchair.

More examinations needed to be carried out before the diagnosis could be officially confirmed. Owen then had a battery of tests, including more blood samples, as well as X-rays, electrode tests and ultrasounds. An appointment with Dr Thomas was made for the following month.

The whole family was devastated by the news they received that day. The implications of little Owen having such a severe condition were terrifying. Kim was still in Qatar and everyone tried hard to support her from afar. For the first few days after her son's diagnosis she was so upset that she couldn't even speak to anyone. Will later described how difficult that time was. 'Kim was on the other side of the world and missing Owen and me, so she wasn't in a good place anyway. Then she looked up the syndrome on Google, which was probably the worst thing she could have done because she saw that there is often a life expectancy of only twelve years. That completely panicked her. She felt so helpless so far away and she'd cry on the phone, convinced that Owen would have a shortened life. The RAF was great and gave her extended phone cards so that we could discuss it for longer, but there was nothing either of us could do but wait.'

Kim flew home for some R&R and the couple wanted to see Dr Thomas together, so Will rang his office and offered to pay privately to see him. The consultant dropped everything and saw them the next day. He told them then that he was 99 per cent certain that Owen had Schwartz-Jampel syndrome, and confirmed that there was no known cure. All he and his team could do was prescribe a series of medicines to try to reduce Owen's muscle stiffness. He went on to explain that the syndrome occurs only when faulty chromosomes in both parents happen to match up. Even though there were no serious health issues on either side of their family, everyone carries a few faulty genes and Will and Kim both happened to have a defective tenth chromosome. For two people to have the same faulty genes is extremely rare. 'We didn't know it when we tried for a child, but it was like the *Titanic* and the iceberg coming together,' said Will. 'There was a one in two million chance of two people with exactly the same faulty gene connecting, and something like a one in four billion chance of us having a child with the syndrome.'

Dr Thomas told Will and Kim that there was one way

to make absolutely sure that Owen had Schwartz-Jampel syndrome and that was to cut out a tiny piece of his skin – the size of a grain of rice – and send it to specialist laboratories in France. It would then take up to six months to compare and analyse all the chromosomes and genes in samples of their blood with those from Owen's sample to get a definitive result.

Will was away on a training course when Kim went with Owen, her parents and her sister Katie to have the skin plug harvested and some electrode tests to his nerves. The experience was, they said, 'horrendous'. Owen used to say that his best friend was his Granddad Hugh (who was known as his 'Whoop-Whoop' Granddad because of his job in the police), but he wasn't his best friend that day. Hugh Knott, who'd been in the Royal Marines, had to clamp down on Owen to keep him still as he screamed. Kim became so distressed that she was almost physically sick and had to leave the room.

The prospect of facing a lifetime of living with a rare syndrome affected Owen's parents very differently. They were both shattered to think that there was no treatment to cure their son's condition and that he faced years of pain. Kim was deployed back to Qatar, but Will was home with Owen for almost every medical appointment after that, which gave him more time to get used to the idea. Frustrated with waiting for the clinic results from France, though, and after doing some research on the internet, he asked to be referred to Great Ormond Street Children's Hospital for a second opinion. Kim's parents and Aunt Laura went along for moral support.

Like many people, Will believed that Great Ormond Street Hospital was the best in the world for sick kids and he desperately wanted the advice of their doctors. The family waited for hours while Owen had a series of tests and eventually the doctors asked Will about the care Owen had had already. When he told them that his son was under the supervision of Dr Thomas at Southampton Hospital, they asked him, 'What are you doing here? He's the best in the country!' So Will had to go back to Southampton with his tail between his legs, but of course Dr Thomas understood that he was just a dad trying to do the best for his little boy.

When Kim returned home from her posting, she and Will bought their son a walker and tried to coax him into using it by decorating it in the same green as his favourite Ben 10 cartoon character. They adorned it with lights and stickers, but Owen still seemed extremely reluctant to use it or to attempt to walk on his own.

Kim and Will swapped roles as he was dispatched to Iraq for three months, so it was Kim who took Owen back to Southampton Hospital for Owen's final test results. 'When they told us the diagnosis was confirmed I broke down,' said Kim. 'It seemed so cruel. I remember crying and telling my mum that Owen would never splash in the puddles or have a normal Sunday with us as a family, with a roast dinner followed by an afternoon kicking a ball around the garden with his dad.'

Will felt much the same way. 'You want to see your child

run about the park. You want to play football with your son. It hit me very hard then that that was something that was never going to happen.'

Badly shaken, Kim became depressed and went to see an occupational psychotherapist at work. She recommended that Will speak to someone as well when he returned from Iraq. He later said that at first he only went along because he wanted to be sure he wasn't going crazy, but in fact the therapist helped him realize that what he was feeling was normal. He wasn't depressed, but was going through 'a major adjustment to a lifestyle change'. She also helped him look at the positives – there were two possibilities with the syndrome and Owen had the better of them.

Once his tour of duty in Iraq was over, Will tried to focus on the positives, which wasn't always easy because Owen had started falling over a lot. His mobility was poor, his balance was shot and his muscles were becoming increasingly tense. Because they never relaxed, it was almost impossible for him to put out his arms to save himself, so he tended to hurt himself whenever he fell. Kim was with Owen in a restaurant when he slipped off a bench and cut his head open. There was blood everywhere, and she had to call an ambulance. Something similar happened at his nursery, and he got a black eye when his grandparents' Springer Spaniel accidentally tripped him up. 'When he falls, he falls like a tree trunk,' said Kim, 'because he can't bend to save himself, despite my dad showing him how to do Commando rolls!'

Everyone had to be on constant alert. Kim's overwhelming desire was to mollycoddle Owen, but she and the rest of the family tried to avoid that, even though it often broke them not to. 'People often say to me, "It could be worse," and I tell them, "Yes, but it could be a whole bloody lot better too!" It isn't easy having a disabled child.'

Some of Owen's problems have come as a direct result of his diagnosis. Because of the syndrome's rarity, there are no treatments specifically tailored to its many effects. Anti-convulsive medications used for epilepsy and other conditions are usually all that can be prescribed.

When the syndrome was first confirmed, Owen could manage to climb up and down stairs and manoeuvre outside in his bubble car by wheeling himself around. This changed after he was prescribed a strong muscle-relaxant. Will found out later that some of the side-effects of that particular medication include drowsiness, constipation and damage to vision. The drug can also affect balance.

'Owen had been in some pain – crying and whining and holding himself rigid,' explained Will. 'The medication helped reduce that pain so we had no choice but to keep him on it, even though I suspected it was doing him harm. We were caught between a rock and a hard place.'

Owen had regular physiotherapy and occupational therapy (only some of which was government funded) and his walking frame helped propel him along. In the early days, he'd walk up a hill to nursery and home again. He'd lift his legs on the way home and wheel himself back down the hill. Then his parents bought him a fold-down stool with casters and that made life easier for him at home, but when he went to nursery he tried to keep up with the other children tearing around the playground by running on his toes in his frame. Will believes that the combination of his medication and being on tiptoes affected his balance and shortened his calf muscles. Owen then had to wear splints on his feet and lower legs at night to try to stretch them out. It was a new and unwelcome development.

Caring for Owen full-time and being separated from each other for months on end put an inevitable strain on Will and Kim's marriage and the couple eventually sought counselling. 'We both recognized there were problems and we tried to sort them out,' said Will. 'Neither of us are the type of people to give up, and I come from a strong Christian background in which I had always been taught to work at staying together.'

In 2008, Kim was sent to Afghanistan while Will stayed at home to look after their son. He worked day shifts while Owen was cared for in the nursery or by family members. The couple had a lot on their minds and things weren't right between them. They had drifted apart. There was no one else involved and neither of them ever thought they'd end up divorcing, but during a series of long chats on the telephone they eventually agreed that it would be better if they separated. Although the decision was devastating for them both, their next priority had to be what was best for Owen.

The biggest shock for Will was the thought of not being with his son all the time. From day one, he'd been the one who mostly got up at night to feed Owen. He'd let Kim recover from the birth and then from her post-natal depression, and even after she was fine and back at work he had carried on feeding and caring for his son. 'Kim's a fantastic mum and it never even occurred to me that I might get custody of Owen, because mothers always seem to get the children in a divorce,' he said. 'But then I spoke to a lawyer who told me that wasn't necessarily the case – especially as I'd been Owen's principal carer. I was advised not to leave the house, but to move into the spare room and, if necessary, let a judge decide.'

When Kim returned from Afghanistan just before Christmas 2008 and Will told her he believed that he had as much right to Owen as she did, the news hit her, she says, 'like a juggernaut'. She had assumed that Will would just move out of the RAF house they shared and that would be the end of it. Stunned by his announcement, she stayed up all night crying. The following morning, exhausted and feeling unable to remain under the same roof as her estranged husband, Kim packed her bags and left.

Both of them knew it was never an option to remove Owen from the only home he'd ever known.

Kim explained, 'I went a bit off the rails when we split up. It was so very shocking to me because I thought that, as Owen's mum, it would be me who'd be awarded custody of him. At the same time, though, I knew Will was a brilliant father – in many ways better at parenting than me.' She didn't know what to do for the best, or how she would cope with being the twenty-six-year-old single mum to a disabled child and working full-time. Even though her parents and her sister Katie were a huge part of Owen's life and had always helped with his care, she still knew that her responsibilities would be enormous. She underwent a course of counselling, and then she was promoted and offered a posting to Oxford.

That was when she made the decision to do what was best for Owen.

'I wasn't running away,' she said. 'I was only going to be thirty miles up the road and I would see him all the time – but it seemed like a clean break. It was the most difficult decision I have ever had to make in my life – and I have always felt judged by people for it – but at that point I knew it would be best if I stepped aside and let Will take care of our son.'

Will and his family have nothing but praise for Kim. 'She made the greatest sacrifice a mother can possibly make,' Will said. 'She loves Owen and is still a huge and vitally important part of his life – as are all her family – but she realized it was best for our son if he stayed with me.'

The couple even worked out their divorce themselves through a self-help organization to save time, money and distress. In February 2009 Kim signed off everything and let Will have primary custody of Owen.

Although Will had got what he wanted, the reality took

time to set in. When it did, the whole prospect was very daunting. He had been hoping for promotion at work and was in line for what he thought of as his 'dream job', but, after weeks of agonizing, he gave all that up, turning his back on furthering his career in order to be the best father he could be to Owen. He admits that there was a moment when he thought 'Bloody hell – what have I let myself in for?' and when he went to see his recruiting officer to inform him of the situation the response was 'Let her have him!' The senior officer at first told Will that he was doing a stupid thing, but finally he admitted that he could understand his reasons why.

To complicate matters – and as the divorce was still being finalized – Will was deployed to Afghanistan for four months and Kim learned that she was soon to be sent to Kenya for two months on exercises. Nevertheless, she offered to move back into their home to take care of Owen while Will was away – with the help of both sets of grand-parents – until she went overseas and he got back. Her sister Katie also helped out and, around the same time, her parents moved from their Devonshire three-storey town-house into a chalet bungalow with a ramp so that Owen could stay with them too. They and Kim began to organize charity events, including a half-marathon, a pasty-bake, a raffle and a cupcake sale to raise money for a new £8,500 Zippie wheelchair for Owen to use while he was in their care. The Royal Marines alone collected £400 by shaking buckets in the street and at their own events.

Will and Kim will always be grateful for the way their

friends and family rallied round to help them, just as they always had. Whatever had happened between them, everyone's prime concern was still for Owen.

The soon-to-be Corporal Will Howkins heard that the divorce court had issued his decree absolute as he was waiting to fly out of RAF Brize Norton in Oxfordshire. With more pressing matters on his mind, he informed his lawyer that the paperwork would have to wait.

As he left the UK to serve Queen and country, strapped into the belly of a Hercules C-130 troop carrier, he wondered what the future would hold for him and his son. He could only hope for the best.

He could never have imagined what lay in wait.

3

'Love is like a butterfly. The more you chase it, the more it will elude you. But if you turn your attention towards other things it will come and softly sit on your shoulder.'

Unknown

COLLEEN DRUMMOND IS the first to admit she isn't technically minded. So when well-meaning girl-friends posted her details and photograph on an online dating website in the summer of 2009, they knew she wouldn't even know how to unsubscribe.

The thirty-eight-year-old New Zealander had never considered using any dating sites before – the whole idea terrified her. She had the impression that they were only for people who were desperate and was convinced she'd be scammed or lured into a date with a psychopath. Her girl-friends insisted it was no different to meeting someone in a bar, but she rarely drinks and wasn't the type to go to bars anyway.

Insisting that Colleen had been single for too long,

however, her friends persuaded her to let them create a profile for her on the dating site of their choice and they posted a photo of her with an aggressive-looking Malinois or Belgian Shepherd dog. The dog was Colleen's own idea. 'Her name was Alpha and she was a real beauty,' she explained, 'but she also had a look that said, "I'll kill you if you hurt my mum."'

The day after her profile appeared, Colleen checked her dating page and discovered a smiley face, which indicated that someone liked the look of her and wanted to make contact. At first she panicked, but when the 'smiler's' profile stated that his name was Will, he was thirty-one, had a son and was working abroad. She assumed that he probably just wanted a pen-pal so she plucked up her courage and sent a smiley face back. Little did she know that she and her admirer lived only nine miles apart and that they even used the same supermarket.

Colleen, who grew up in Hokitika on South Island in New Zealand, came from a broken home and had little contact with her father after he left when she was five years old. Her mother, Kathryn, worked hard as a psychiatric nurse to provide for her three young children. For some of her childhood Colleen and her siblings were raised by their grandparents, Sylvia and Bruce, with some invaluable help and guidance from her free-spirited Aunt Tui, who had never married or had children of her own but regarded her nieces and nephew as her own. As the eldest child, Colleen became head of the household. She was cooking the family meals by the age of eight, by thirteen she had a job washing hair in a salon to bring in some extra cash, and at seventeen she left home to find work in Australia and to travel. Having done everything from filing to cleaning hotel bedrooms, she arrived in London in the mid-1990s and ended up sharing a flat with some fellow 'Kiwis'. Soon afterwards she got a job in a West End department store and quickly progressed to a management position, but – missing the fresh air and open spaces of her youth – she was desperate to find work outdoors.

She had always loved dogs – her mother used to show Staffordshire Bull Terriers when Colleen was a little girl – so in the summer of 2000 she switched careers and applied for a job training and working with dogs in Surrey.

Having been married and then divorced quite young soon after arriving in the UK, Colleen had since been involved in a couple of failed relationships, but now she'd been single for two years. She had bought herself a house in Aldershot, in Hampshire, and had what she called 'a nice enough life', but she figured she was probably destined to be on her own. To her mind, dogs seemed far more loyal than men and were a lot easier to deal with, so when the internet stranger on the other side of the world whom she knew only as Will sent her a smiley face, she still didn't expect it to lead to anything more than an electronic friendship.

He seemed keener, however, and suggested she buy a webcam and set up Skype. He quickly discovered that she had no knowledge of computers, so he talked her through the process via emails. Because of the sensitive nature of where he was based, he explained that they would only be able to see each other on camera and would have to type all their messages because there could be no sound.

The first time Will's face popped up on Colleen's screen she was pleasantly surprised. He looked cute and wasn't at all her 'type' – which had always been blonds or men with shaved heads. Smiling and waving to each other, they started chatting online and got along surprisingly well.

Will's first thought was 'She'll do!' and he really looked forward to their chats. The experience changed his view of dating websites. He'd signed up to a few after his divorce from Kim but was growing increasingly disillusioned. There were a couple of women he made contact with that he described as 'horrors' and one he dubbed 'Miss Liar', so in the end he couldn't be bothered with it.

The day after Colleen's profile was posted online by her friends was the day he'd logged on to cancel his sub-scription to that particular site. When he did, he found a message waiting for him from a woman whose profile he dismissed, and then thought that while he was logged in he'd give it one last shot to see who else was out there. When he spotted blonde Colleen and her impressive-looking dog he thought there was something about her. Taking a deep breath, he sent her a smiley. He told himself that if she didn't respond within twenty-four hours he would go ahead and unsubscribe as planned.

Unbeknownst to Colleen, she was on a deadline.

The couple continued to meet and chat online over the next five weeks – quite often at what they called 'stupid o'clock' because of the time difference or their shift patterns. The more Colleen got to know Will, the more she liked him, but only as a friend at first. She had connected with a few other men online too – purely as friends – but couldn't get Will out of her head.

Will felt the same way, but he sensed her suspicions about dating sites generally. Determined to prove that he was genuine, he started to open up about himself a bit more, although he held back from telling her about Owen's condition.

Colleen was still a little wary. Will was younger than she was and had a son who lived with him, which was just the kind of baggage she didn't want. Still, there was something about him that she was really drawn to.

When Colleen was invited out on a date by one of her other online pen-pals based in the UK, she was petrified, but her girlfriends told her she'd have to take the plunge at some stage, so she reluctantly agreed to say yes. Even so, she texted one of her friends as soon as she left the house and again when she arrived at the restaurant – just in case her dinner companion turned out to be an axe murderer. As she walked in to meet him for the first time she felt sick to her stomach.

The blind date didn't go well, and when Colleen returned home that night she realized the first person she wanted to talk to was Will.

She was surprised to be feeling guilty, because even

though they spoke every day she hadn't told him that she was going on a date. Although there'd been no hint of taking their relationship further, she still felt as if she'd somehow cheated on him.

'He was online,' she related later, 'and he asked me where I'd been, so I told him. That's when his face hit the floor. Then I recounted what a disaster it had been and as I was typing the story, I could see that he was peeing himself laughing.

'When I typed, "I don't know why I'm telling you this because I'm not your girlfriend," inside I thought, "Damn – I have feelings for you!"'

'Then he typed, "I have something to confess . . . I really like you."'

'I responded, "You could've told me!"'

'He wrote, "Well you could've warned me you were going on a date!"'

A few minutes after they finished chatting Colleen received a telephone call on her mobile that came up with an unknown UK prefix. She answered it cautiously and heard a very posh voice say, 'Hi, it's Will.'

She only knew one Will and he was in Afghanistan, not in the UK. Immediately she had visions that he was really a psycho sitting in a fake Afghanistan setting deceiving her on the internet. He immediately guessed what she was thinking from her stunned reaction and assured her that his switchboard had patched his call through from his HQ. She was enormously relieved.

That was the first time they'd heard each other's voices.

They had already fallen for each other online and now they began to fall in love on the telephone as well. Before long neither of them could wait for Will to come home.

He was due to fly back to the UK on 14 August 2009 and they'd arranged to meet for dinner that night in Farnham, in Surrey. Before he came home he finally told her everything – that he'd been married, divorced, and that his son was disabled – so that she still had 'a chance to run away', he said. He made it clear that he was looking for someone he could have fun with, and not searching for a mother for Owen. 'He already has an awesome mum whom he loves very much,' he told Colleen. 'This relationship would be for weekends and fun nights out.'

Because of Colleen's history, she didn't believe there was such a thing as a good dad, and certainly not a good single dad. To find out that Will had taken on the care of his disabled son 'gobsmacked' her. 'I thought if he was that loyal to a little disabled boy then I couldn't ask for better. This wasn't a part-time dad. This was a real father, and I'd been looking for one of those all my life.'

On the day the couple was due to meet Colleen had her hair done and then set off for their romantic rendezvous. She took along her favourite Beatrix Potter bracelet to wear. She'd always loved Beatrix Potter, who, as a sheep farmer, was what she called 'a New Zealander in the wrong hemisphere'. Living on her own, Colleen couldn't put the bracelet on by herself, so she parked a little early at the supermarket car park where they'd agreed to meet and asked a stranger for help. The woman looked at her as if she was crazy and replied that she was in a hurry. She must have seen Colleen's face fall because then she stopped and asked, 'What's it for?' When Colleen confessed she was on a blind date and the bracelet was her lucky charm the woman cried, 'Give it here!' and fastened it for her.

Colleen didn't know that Will – who had only been back in the UK for a few hours – was already parked and waiting to meet his girlfriend for the first time. He watched the whole episode with the bracelet and his first thought was that she'd brought her mother with her. When the Good Samaritan eventually wandered off, wishing her luck, though, he beeped his car horn and waved.

As he got out of the car, tanned and fit after his recent tour of duty, Colleen stopped in her tracks and said to herself, 'Wow! I've just met my husband!' She felt that the connection between them was as instantaneous as that.

The couple had a lovely dinner together and stayed chatting so late in the restaurant that the staff had to ask them to leave so that they could close. They met again a few days later and – in a way they both described as 'very old-fashioned' – took time to get to know each other better.

Will didn't plan to introduce Colleen to Owen until he was completely sure that she intended to stick around, but ten days later it was his son's fourth birthday – one day after Colleen's – so he invited his new girlfriend to meet his son.

She was understandably nervous. She had never wanted kids herself; she didn't really feel that her lifestyle suited children and thought it just wasn't for her. Although most of her friends were married with families, what had happened to her own mum had also put her off completely.

The day Colleen first met Owen he was sitting in his special chair with a little fluffy cushion and she thought he was the cutest thing she had ever seen. She was determined not to overreact or throw herself all over him, which she suspected would only scare him. Nor did she want to go rushing in and step on anyone's toes. 'He is Kim's son and she's a perfectly good mother. It is not my job to be his mother. It is my job just to be Colleen.'

With little experience of children, Colleen said she tended to treat them as she would her dogs – by rewarding good behaviour. 'I just said to Owen, "Hello, mate. Happy birthday, little buddy. Can I sit next to you?" He nodded and smiled at me and let me cuddle up to him. From that day on he was my "Little Buddy" – hence his nickname, Little B.'

Colleen had been determined to buy Owen a birthday gift but didn't know what he liked, so she asked Will's advice. The response was, 'Anything with Ben 10 on it.' So she went to Toys 'R' Us and asked someone to direct her to the Ben 10 aisle, even though she still had no idea what it was (Ben 10 is a little boy with a magic watch that turns him into an alien). She eventually picked out a remote-controlled car because it had a big round controller instead of a stick, which she thought might be better for Owen's hands. On his birthday she gave him his present and was amazed by his reaction. He put her gift down on the table and carefully opened his card first, pretending to read it (even though he couldn't yet). Then he opened his present, gently lifting the Sellotape and being careful not to spoil the paper. 'He was so sweet and thoughtful and polite,' said Colleen, 'that from that moment on, he was sold to the woman sitting next to him!'

The pair got along famously and Will was so relieved that he asked Colleen out on what he called a 'proper' date the following week. In the lavender garden of Waddesdon Manor in Buckinghamshire, he told her that he loved her.

Even though she felt exactly the same way, the couple still took things slowly and decided to tread carefully. There was a lot for both of them to consider.

The next time Colleen saw 'Little B' it was at Will's parents' house; it was the first time she had met them and she got along with them immediately. She walked into their lounge where Owen was playing on the floor and said, 'Goodday, mate, how are you?'

Looking up, he cried out, 'Colleeeen!' and crawled along the furniture to put his arms out to her. Colleen recalled, 'I just melted in a puddle of Anchor butter.'

As they fell more deeply in love, Colleen started to stay overnight at Will's home in Odiham. She was there when Owen fell down the stairs one night, which gave them all a fright. Then he did it again.

The couple discovered that he had taught himself to flip over in bed and get out of his room because he wanted to walk 'like a big boy'. They could hear his hands tap-tap-tapping on the wall if he came in to see them. Then one day he tried the stairs because he wanted to go down and prepare breakfast for them as a surprise. He wasn't yet five years old.

Colleen couldn't bear the idea of Owen falling again. A couple of days later she put her house on the market and told Will they were buying a bungalow together. They'd only known each other for a few months but he knew she was right.

Keen to include Owen in every decision that impacted on his life, they took him along to view some properties and when they found the one in Basingstoke to which they would eventually move he walked in and cried, 'Yay! No stairs!' The bungalow would require a lot of renovating before they could all move in together, but the decision was made. They were going to be a family.

Although Owen had started at primary school and seemed to be getting along all right with his fellow pupils, his family noticed that he was beginning to become increasingly withdrawn. Having been protected by them for years, he had suddenly come face to face with children the same age who were fully mobile and running around, whereas he could move around only by holding on to the walls. He couldn't stand up by himself and was relying on his walker more and more. Often during playtime he had to remain inside his classroom for fear of being knocked over. Will recognized that, although his son was too young to put it into words, he was beginning to realize there were some things his friends could do now, such as learning how to play football, that he would never be able to do and he was really taking it to heart. He had always been bright and funny and quite observant, but now he was retreating into himself and it was hard for his father to know what to do to bring him out of his shell.

Will hoped that if Little B could only have more mobility then he might not feel quite so left out. He made the tough and deeply emotional decision to apply for a wheelchair for him from the local health authority, which seemed 'a huge step'. Unfortunately, the authority ruled that as Owen could occasionally walk (with assistance), he didn't qualify for more than the basic NHS model, which was heavy, cumbersome and very difficult to manoeuvre. Owen himself, however, made it easier for everyone by showing great excitement about having what he called a 'bigger, better buggy', even if it was impossible for him to move it by himself and it jolted him badly every time it went over a bump, giving him headaches.

Just as he got used to his new machine and seemed to be making some friends at school, though, he had a growth spurt that caused his spasms to tighten his facial features even more. His eyes started narrowing and the muscles on his body became even more pronounced. Will observed how 'People really took notice of him, and when he cottoned on to the fact that they were looking at him he began to put his head down. He hated people staring at him and the more they did, the more he hid away.'

Before long, Little B no longer wanted to go out in public. Whenever Will told him they were going to the park or the shops, he'd protest. When his father insisted, Owen would beg him to carry him instead. It broke Will's heart to tell him he was too heavy for that. He had no choice but to strap his son into the wheelchair and take him out anyway, but he hated it and would get very upset. Owen's typical pose once they were out of the house became head down, arms in and curled in on himself.

On other occasions Owen told Kim, 'People are looking at me and I don't like it!' At first she tried to persuade him that it was because he was 'so adorable'; then she explained that it was no different to him staring at one of the disabled servicemen they sometimes saw on the base: 'You might look at them,' she told him, 'but that doesn't mean you don't like them. It's just that they're a little bit different.' In the end she had to tell her son that some people just didn't understand.

Owen's grandmother Joan took him to her local church with her at least once a month and, although he enjoyed the services and connected well with some of the congregation, a lot of the time he remained very withdrawn and hid his face from view, completely disconnecting himself and putting up a barrier. Only if someone came right up to him and engaged with him did he let his guard down and respond.

Colleen also did everything she could to encourage her little buddy, but he started clamming up in public and was clearly not coping at all well with how others viewed his disability. Some people were rude and insensitive, and stared so openly that Colleen sometimes asked them bluntly, 'Do you want to take a picture too?'

Within a short space of time, however, she had more pressing matters on her mind. Having mourned the death of her beloved grandmother Sylvia in 2009, she now lost her grandfather Bruce. The couple had been happily married for over sixty years – ever since they were teenagers – and had been her inspiration and comfort throughout her childhood. Colleen was devastated by the double loss.

Then, soon after her grandfather died, her dog Alpha started behaving strangely around her – pawing at her and sniffing. It became such an issue that, although she felt completely well, she went to her doctor and asked her to run some tests because she'd heard of cases where dogs had alerted their owners to something medically wrong. Sure enough, the tests detected pre-cancerous cells and she was booked in almost straight away for a hysterectomy.

With Colleen needing gentle nursing after her surgery, Will was able to show her what a natural carer he was. Realizing that she'd be off work for several weeks, the couple decided it was a good time to get a rescue dog. Will had grown up with a Flat-coated Retriever named Jessie and loved having Colleen's work animals around, and they both hoped that having a dog of his own might be good for Owen. The one they chose was a Spaniel-Collie cross puppy that they named Mr Pixel. However, although Little B loved Mr Pixel, he never bonded with him in the way the couple had hoped and he still wasn't keen on going out in his wheelchair to take him for a walk.

Weak and on crutches after her surgery, Colleen

nevertheless decided to take Will on holiday in July 2010 to thank him for taking such good care of her. Her grandfather had left her a little money in his will so she used it to book them a week in Scotland, in a tree house on the Kinlochlaich Estate near Fort William.

As soon as Colleen told Will that she was taking him away, he decided that this would be the perfect time to ask her to marry him. She was keeping their destination a secret, so he decided to surprise her too. Secretly, he started looking online for engagement rings – but one night she spotted what he was looking at on his computer and burst into tears of joy.

Will had chosen a ring of rose and white gold with butterflies – her grandmother's favourite creatures, and always very special to Colleen. She was thrilled, but she wanted to see it for herself so they went to the shop together. It was perfect and she couldn't have been happier. Then Will shocked her by asking the assistant to put it to one side until he needed it. He secretly collected it from the shop a week later and kept it hidden until they set off.

On the long drive to Scotland, the butterfly ring felt as if it was burning a hole in his pocket, and by the time they arrived in Fort William, on Saturday 28 July, Will could barely contain his excitement. He made it through Sunday but couldn't think straight – he had to know Colleen's answer. Early on the Monday morning he summoned her outside in the rain and when she asked him why, the tension got to him and he snapped, 'Just do it, woman!'

Colleen later described what happened. 'I was having a rough time after my surgery. I had stitches and was in pain and feeling awful. He dragged me out of the house still drugged up to the eyeballs and I thought he wanted to show me a rare bird.

'The next thing I knew he was down on one knee and I said, "Oh God! What's wrong?" because I thought he'd collapsed. Then I realized what was happening and I started to cry.

'He looked up at me and said, "You know I love you so much and you are wonderful to Owen. Will you marry me?" so I grabbed hold of him and told him that of course I bloody would!'

Colleen couldn't wait to tell someone their news, so she hobbled over to the house of the couple who owned the property and banged on their door. They were the first to know. Will, meanwhile, posted cryptically on Facebook that the views in Scotland were 'very engaging' as Colleen and he floated through the rest of that week.

Will had always made a point of including Owen in any decision that would affect him, so he had already asked his son's permission to propose marriage to Colleen. He asked him how he would feel about having Colleen as his step-mum and Owen shouted out, 'Yes!' He had loved her from day one, so he was delighted.

When Will asked Owen if he would do him the honour of being his best man, the reply was 'Cool!'

Will had also asked Colleen's mother, Kathryn, for her permission by telephone. She had followed her daughter to the UK in 1999 and lived in Gants Hill, in North London, where she still worked as a nurse. She adored Will and Little B, and had never known Colleen so happy, so she was thrilled for them all. Colleen called her younger sister, Charissa, in New Zealand, and brother, Marcus, in Western Australia, and told them the good news. They were both delighted for her.

With the recent purchase of their bungalow – a place that needed months of improvement and modification for Owen before they could move in – money was very tight. The couple knew they'd need time to save up for the kind of wedding they wanted, so they set the date for the summer of 2013. Colleen's lucky number is seventeen, so they picked the only Saturday the 17th they could find – which happened to fall in August. The whole family was looking forward to the big day.

Little B was doing a bit better at school now, but when he was teased a couple of times he started to lash out. One day there was a clash of heads in the playground. Another boy had told him he looked 'funny', so Owen had head-butted him. Will had to go to the school to talk to his son, who initially claimed that his antagonist had slipped and hit his head. They had 'a serious word', and Will told Little B that the only time he could strike out physically was if he was struck first. It hasn't happened since.

No matter how well behaved he was at school or how comfortable he felt with his family or in a place where he knew everyone, Owen was still painfully shy, anxious and

withdrawn in public and didn't want to be 'seen'.
Everyone, from Will and Colleen to Kim and his grandparents, was growing increasingly concerned. His shyness
meant that he wasn't developing socially. He hardly ever
had any friends round to play and he didn't go to other
children's homes much either – probably because their
parents were worried they wouldn't know what to do with
a disabled boy. He was also showing signs of impatience at
having to put on the leg splints he sometimes had to wear,
and at having to take his medication, both of which
required his full cooperation.

He was happiest at home watching TV or in a
restaurant with his family – his local Pizza Express had
become his favourite and he knew exactly what to order
every time. If the family took him anywhere else in public,
though, he was patently unhappy. Once, in a supermarket,
he challenged an old lady who was staring at him and
asked her to stop. When she didn't, he told her she
smelled. Will 'read him the riot act' and told him that he
should always be polite, even if others were being rude,
but Owen's growing awareness of his disability and how
others viewed him was clearly beginning to affect him.

In the hopes of lifting his spirits, Will arranged a fifth
birthday party for his son at the church hall in Odiham.
He told Owen he could have any theme he wanted and the
boy, who often asked for Metallica as his music of prefer-
ence during breakfast, picked 'Rock 'n' Roll', so everyone
had to dress up as a rock star. He asked for a bouncy
castle so that he could watch his friends having fun. 'He

had a fantastic day,' said Will. 'He even went on the bouncy castle and enjoyed being bumped around. I think that was when a lot of the other kids and their parents realized that Little B could party just as hard as they could. It was a real eye-opener for them to see him behaving like any normal little boy in a social environment.'

Later that year, Will found out that he was to be deployed on his second tour of duty to Afghanistan – as part of the team servicing and maintaining the Chinook helicopters. It meant that he would be away from home for what he and Colleen both describe as the worst Christmas of their lives.

With Colleen working full-time, including night shifts, Will's parents offered to move into his house at Odiham to help care for Owen. On a day out, Joan took her grandson to Chichester Cathedral and was amazed by the little boy's reaction to the beauty and serenity of the building, which he had never seen before. He suddenly spotted a little chapel with candles flickering; it was off to one side and behind some gates. He asked his grandmother if they could go in and light a candle and pray for Will. Joan was very touched; it was only later that she discovered it was the Chapel of St Clement and contained a Memorial to the Fallen, complete with the RAF emblem. Owen hadn't been able to see that from where they were when he first asked to light the candle, but his grandmother felt it was as if he was drawn there somehow.

It was Kim's turn to have Little B that Christmas, so Will's parents invited Colleen to spend it with them at their home in Midhurst in West Sussex. Will's brother, Ed, and sisters, Esther and Bethany, were there too, along with their respective partners and children. Everyone missed Will, though. He rang on Christmas Day in the middle of their roast turkey lunch. There had been a lot of blackouts in Camp Bastion that month and it had been a much tougher tour for him this time. Colleen put him on loud-speaker at the dinner table so that the family could hear his voice, but when he heard everyone wishing him Merry Christmas he became very emotional.

Colleen rushed off into another room with the phone so that she could talk privately with him. When Joan went to see if she was all right, she burst into tears too because she found that her future daughter-in-law had been cry-ing so hard she'd made her nose bleed. That tour of duty was the first time she and Will had been apart and it made Colleen realize that being in love with a member of the armed forces isn't easy, especially when they're deployed to danger zones.

And she had another fear. 'I was worried sick about Will's safety, of course, but my other huge concern was that if anything happened to him I wouldn't just lose the love of my life, I'd lose the boy who was the closest I'd ever have to a son. The courts would automatically give Kim parental rights – as they should, she's his mother. But it really made me fearful of what could happen.'

Colleen wasn't just concerned about her own needs. She knew Little B desperately needed his daddy. The bond between them had made them virtually inseparable. If anything happened to Will, and with Kim working away so much, Colleen feared that Owen might be passed from one long-suffering member of the family to the next.

Trying not to dwell on the worst-case scenario, she could do nothing but wait for Will to come back, which he did, safely, in February 2011, much to everyone's relief.

The couple could finally set about making a cosy home for Owen, themselves and Mr Pixel (along with Colleen's two working dogs, who lived in purpose-built kennels in their new garden).

They were also able to focus more of their attention on Owen, who now needed regular physiotherapy and hydrotherapy as well as frequent visits to a chiropractor. The muscle contractions in his face were pinching his features and narrowing his eyelids, making it more and more difficult for him to see; the doctors told Will that they might eventually have to operate on the lids in order to keep his eyes open. Coupled with that, his eyesight had also deteriorated – partly due to his medication – and he needed prescription glasses. Owen was also undergoing frequent sleep studies at Southampton Hospital to check his oxygen intake. The spasms in his chest had worsened, which meant that when he lay down to sleep, the tightening muscles crushed his chest and stopped him from breathing easily. The consequence was that he kept waking up to cough – sometimes as many as fifty times in one night. He had also developed asthma because he couldn't fully expand his ribcage. This caused his blood oxygen levels to drop – something known as hypoxia – which could potentially damage his heart or his brain.

At first, Will and Colleen worried that dog hair might be affecting Owen, but they were assured it wasn't an issue with his particular problem. He had coughed from a young age (before he had contact with dogs) and coughing was a recognized symptom of his syndrome.

Dr Thomas at Southampton admitted that Owen's breathing was a 'cause for concern'; the muscle stiffness was adversely affecting his breathing muscles to the point that he couldn't clear his chest or take a breath to the depth of his chest. This left him more at risk of chest infections and the treatments were very limited.

Owen's medical team had little choice but to prescribe an oxygen mask for him at night, which meant that a specialist company had to fit an airflow machine in his bedroom. They also had to deliver the oxygen cylinders, which could only be transported legally by registered providers. They came with all sorts of warnings about not smoking near them and being careful to keep them stable.

The oxygen helped, although Little B didn't like the nasal mask attached to a tube, or the tape required to hold it in place. Will had to set his alarm and get up four or five times a night to check that the mask was still in place or his son might start to choke.

Owen's need for oxygen also meant that he could only stay overnight in places where a flow machine and air purifier were already installed. Otherwise they'd have to be set up especially for him, including for any holidays or trips away. Both sets of grandparents had the necessary equipment installed in their homes so that he could stay with them, but Kim had more of a problem.

The RAF had always been extremely accommodating to her and to Will about their son's needs. Over the years, they had repeatedly given the couple time off for hospital and other medical appointments and couldn't have been more understanding. That was, until Kim moved out of the family home and needed suitable quarters of her own.

The Ministry of Defence doesn't officially recognize joint custody of a child when it comes to allocating housing. With Will listed as the primary carer, Kim had no choice but to move into an RAF bedsit in 'the block' – a purpose-built block of flats on the airbase – which didn't even have its own private bathroom. As Owen's mother, she still needed a place of stability where he could have his oxygen and a few of his things around him when he came to stay. Although he wasn't living with her full-time, he was still with her over many weekends and she felt that her needs were exactly the same as Will's, who was about to give up his RAF quarters anyway.

After a lengthy battle with the MoD, Kim was finally allocated a surplus house in Bordon, in Hampshire, not far from Basingstoke, where she could safely have Owen to stay. Its 'surplus' status meant that no permanent modifications, such as ramps or grab-handles, could be installed and she could still be kicked out with just a month's notice if the RAF suddenly needed it for someone else; however, Kim's victory at least gave her a place to have her son to herself when she wasn't deployed abroad. She had also found happiness with a fellow serviceman named Lee, a divorced father of two.

Will too was relieved that Kim finally had a proper place of her own. 'Kim is an awesome mother who spoils Little B rotten. She spends as much time with him as she can when she's in the UK, and tries to have him at least twice a month as well as holidays. She's his mum and he loves her to pieces.'

Will and Colleen, meanwhile, were both working hard to pay for their new bungalow and save up for their wedding, as well as looking after Owen. In spite of their hectic lives, however, their thoughts turned to increasing their family. They were considering getting a canine companion for Mr Pixel and had the idea of rescuing another dog. Although they had to think about it very carefully because of Little B, Colleen knew a great deal about training dogs and how to correct bad behaviour, so she didn't think there was much that she couldn't handle.

Ideally, Colleen wanted to find a dog that was already in a foster home rather than a kennel environment. She and Will were looking for something of a similar size to Mr Pixel, or smaller – possibly a King Charles Spaniel, a West Highland Terrier or a Cocker Spaniel.

Unable to bear viewing potential candidates at rescue centres because she knew she'd want to take at least one dog home, she searched online for about three months on the various websites, including those belonging to the RSPCA, the Dogs Trust and Battersea Dogs Home.

Although they spotted a few lovely animals that desperately needed homes, she and Will kept their options open and knew that it was important not to rush.

A few years previously Colleen had done some training with animal behaviourist Ross McCarthy through his London Dog Behaviour Company. She was aware that he'd set up a doggy daycare business called Dogs and Kisses with his partner James Hearle and she followed them both on Facebook.

One night in January 2012 she was sitting on the sofa next to Will scrolling through the pages of Dogs and Kisses when she saw a face looking back at her on the computer and she gasped.

The intense gaze of an Anatolian Shepherd bored straight through her.

Looking up, Will saw Colleen's expression and said, 'Oh no – what have you found?' She didn't say a word – she couldn't speak. She just turned the computer around to face him.

Will took one look at those puppy-dog eyes and said, 'Darn!' They both instantly realized that he was the one for them. All they knew about him at that point was that his name was Haatchi.

Before Will could say another word, Colleen had grabbed her phone and was texting Ross to ask if she could meet the dog she'd just fallen in love with online. Will – who'd met his fiancée online and knew her only too well – just lay back on the sofa with Owen and began to laugh.

4

'Whoever said money can't buy happiness forgot about puppies.'

Gene Hill

COLLEEN ONLY DISCOVERED that Haatchi had lost a leg when she read a little bit more about him on the Dogs and Kisses Facebook page. It made her feel sick to her stomach when she eventually found out how.

All she was told to begin with, though, was that he had been hit by a train. Her chief concern was that his owners might still be looking for him somewhere, but she was assured that it had been weeks since the accident and no one had come forward. Nor was he microchipped, so his family couldn't be traced.

The dog's disability hardly bothered her or Will at all. They were much more worried about his size and temperament around Little B. Having lived and worked with German Shepherds for years, Colleen wasn't fazed by what she read up about Haatchi's breed, but she did need to meet him herself to assess how aggressive he might be.

She couldn't wait.

There were procedures to be carried out before she could, though – the first of which was to fill in a formal adoption form for the UKGSR, which was handling any adoption requests. She answered all their questions but was frustrated that there was no room for any extra comments. Still, she gave them all the information they required, which included the fact that she and Will both worked.

A few days later, she was standing on a freezing-cold airfield training some dogs when her phone vibrated into life. Ross of Dogs and Kisses had forwarded her a copy of the brief email he'd been sent from UKGSR. The response to her application to adopt Haatchi was 'Not suitable.'

She'd been turned down.

The reason given was that Haatchi was likely to be on his own for more than four hours in any given day – but Colleen hadn't been able to explain to the charity that the couple both worked shifts so that would rarely, if ever, happen.

She was mortified. She rang Will and told him, 'We're not getting Haatchi!' He offered to write and explain, but she told him to forget it. 'Maybe it's Fate and it's not meant to be,' she told him, but secretly she was very upset.

An hour later her mobile phone rang. It was Tracey Harris from the UKGSR office telling her they'd just received her email. For a moment she was confused, as she hadn't sent one. That's when she realized Will must have logged on in her name and protested about their decision.

Ross and James had also contacted UKGSR separately, sending what they described as a 'stonking' email, informing the organization that in their professional opinion Colleen and Will were the perfect owners for Haatchi.

Tracey asked Colleen why she'd chosen Haatchi and she replied that her boyfriend was in the RAF and that Haatchi would make a fantastic therapy dog for amputees. Because he looked so big and fluffy, it was something she had been thinking of doing with him right from the start. She added that, from what Ross had told her, Haatchi would be just as relaxed with children as with adults. 'He would also make my stepson smile,' she told Tracey. 'He's disabled and there's just so much of Haatchi to hug.'

Having seen how Mr Pixel's arrival hadn't transformed Owen's life in the way that they'd wished, Colleen secretly didn't hold out too much hope that Haatchi would change anything very much either. She simply prayed it would make her little buddy happier to have a big cuddly bear around.

Once Tracey Harris and UKGSR knew more, they were far more enthusiastic about Colleen adopting Haatchi and arranged for her to visit him a few days later. She drove alone to Ross and James's rambling Oxfordshire country house and found herself in the midst of a zoo of dogs that included several Great Danes, some Pomeranians and even some Chihuahuas.

Ross told her that Haatchi had generated a lot of interest online but that most of it had been from 'unsuitable' owners who wouldn't be able to handle such a large and disabled animal. He'd only agreed for her to visit because he knew that she worked with dogs and would be prepared to put in the time.

'I can be quite clinical about dogs – I have to be,' Colleen said. 'They are the tools of my trade and I can't get too attached. I work with teams of animals that don't make the grade and have to be found homes for. So when I arrived, I was all prepared *not* to fall any more deeply in love with Haatchi.'

As she wandered out into the garden with Ross, her eyes fell upon Claude, a huge Great Dane who was posing like a statue in the middle of the lawn. He stood four square on the grass, but beneath his belly she could see that there was another dog standing behind him – on just three legs.

A big head was staring at her from under Claude's belly with those same two piercing eyes that she had seen on the computer screen. Colleen gasped and took a massive breath, which she then held on to. She had never felt like this about any dog in her life – ever.

'Ross saw me virtually turning blue and he slapped me on the back and cried, "Colleen! Breathe!" I exhaled and clasped my hand to my chest as I gasped for air. The feeling was that overwhelming.'

Ross took Colleen inside to recover and then James brought Haatchi in to meet her. She sat on the sofa as the Anatolian Shepherd staggered in, slipping all over the place because he hadn't got used to having just three legs yet. She slid to the floor and he flopped on top of her and tucked his freckle-covered nose into her neck. He seemed very sad, whining and in obvious pain. She recognized that he craved human attention and that he was very confused.

Ross explained to her that a dog without a tail has great difficulty in communicating with other dogs, because a tail is such a vital tool of communication in many animals. Consequently, it was as if he had lost his voice. Also, the other dogs found the tri-paw strange, both to look at and to smell – his stumps occasionally bled and smelled of disinfectant – so they tended to avoid him.

To make matters worse, Haatchi also suffered from what is known as 'ghost limb' for a while, in which he thought that his missing leg was still there. He'd try to scratch himself behind the ear with it and only end up jerking his stump before whimpering in frustration and pain.

When he finally settled into Colleen's lap, he rolled on to his back and presented her with his leg stump, which was shaved bald and red raw with stitches in it. She asked him gently, 'Can I touch it?' and he didn't seem to mind, so she placed her hand on it and discovered it was really hot. That's when he completely curled himself around her.

All of a sudden James nudged Ross and said, 'Look!'

Haatchi's odd little stump of a tail was wagging – the first time he'd moved it since he went to live with them. Up until then, they told her, they didn't even know if he could.

'From that moment I was sold,' Colleen said later. 'Haatchi had chosen us, not the other way around. There is something truly spiritual about him. I was in love and I knew in my heart that we belonged to him.'

When Colleen got home later that night she burst into tears as she told Will how incredible Haatchi was and how sad she was about what had happened to him. The couple had two weeks to consider whether they were truly prepared to take on such a large, three-legged animal. They needed to be sure they were doing the right thing and for all the right reasons. Owen was Will's priority. He needed to be convinced that a dog who had suffered such cruelty would be safe around his son and he told Colleen that if there was even one growl, then Haatchi was out.

Once they'd made their decision to take Haatchi, they had to pass a UKGSR home check before Colleen would be allowed to collect him. They were a little nervous as their home was inspected and they were asked questions about where Haatchi would be kept and how long he might be left on his own during any given day. Only when they were informed that they had passed the home check was Colleen able to drive back to Oxfordshire to pick up their new baby.

Owen has always loved secrets and surprises, so the couple hadn't told him anything about who was coming to live with them. He was fast asleep in bed by the time Colleen got home with Haatchi late on the night of 18 February, so they closed his bedroom door and let their new dog limp around the house to explore. Then they introduced him to Mr Pixel. Just as they'd hoped, the two dogs got along well and Haatchi showed none of the characteristics so often cited about his breed.

After he had explored every corner of their house and worked out where everything was, Haatchi kept returning to sniff at Owen's bedroom door, so they opened it quietly.

In spite of his injuries, Haatchi – who was still only five months old – was an exuberant puppy, even if one with only three legs. Up until that point, he'd been slipping and sliding all over the house and getting overexcited. The moment he stepped into Owen's bedroom, decorated with *Star Wars* and *Toy Story* murals, all hand-painted by Will, his demeanour completely changed.

As soon as he saw the oxygen mask and the flow machine he sniffed the air repeatedly and almost tiptoed across to where Little B lay. Will and Colleen watched as he tilted his head, as if to say, 'Hmmm, there's something interesting here.' It was if he knew this was a vulnerable little boy and that the machinery and tubes were a no-go area for him. Then he silently backed away.

The following morning, Will woke his son at 7 a.m. and sat on the edge of the bed as his little 'sleep slug' rubbed his eyes and yawned. Will told Owen they had a big surprise for him, and that made him wake up very quickly and become very excited. Then Will invited Colleen to bring Haatchi in. Owen's mouth fell open as a dog three times his size lolloped over and, without any encouragement, placed his head calmly and quietly on Owen's leg. They took one look at each other and each of them melted. It was love at first sight – for both of them.

Colleen said later that the whole atmosphere in the room changed in an instant. 'It was utterly electric – a combination of pure love and acceptance. It is hard to describe the connection between the two of them. It was as if they were reconnecting – like old friends meeting each other again, rather than for the first time. I only wish I'd had a video camera to record the moment.'

What Will found so interesting was that neither boy nor dog backed away from each other or appeared to be in the least bit fazed. Both seemed to realize that there was something unusual about the other. Haatchi wasn't perfect and he wasn't normal, but Owen could see that, although he was so big, he was just getting on with being disabled and didn't let it bother him. Will thought that really struck a chord.

Owen asked what had happened to Haatchi's leg and tail. They didn't want to lie, but it was a hard story both to tell and to hear. Little B cried as they explained as best they could, and all the while he carried on stroking the dog's big head. Overcome with sadness, he asked why anyone would be so cruel. Will and Colleen told him they didn't know, but assured him that the police would catch the person and tell them off. That made him feel a little better.

He got himself up and into his walker and wandered into the living room as Haatchi followed devotedly behind. The two of them curled up together on the sofa, where Owen stroked his new friend some more and began to whisper in his ear. The bond that was forged between them that morning is something that only they will ever understand. For the rest of that weekend boy and dog lay together – in bed, on the sofa or on the floor. Already they were inseparable, and Will and Colleen both knew that Haatchi was there to stay.

'I felt really happy,' Owen said later with a smile. 'Everything changed in my life that day.'

Haatchi had been fed a raw-food diet at Dogs and Kisses and, having read several articles about it being healthier and more natural for dogs, Colleen and Will decided to switch to raw food for him and Mr Pixel. Colleen looked up various companies online and found one called Natural Instinct not too far away in Camberley, in Surrey, so she ordered what she needed from them and asked Will to find them a chest freezer on eBay to keep it all in. He eventually located one but it couldn't be delivered for a few days, so Colleen rang Natural Instinct back and asked them to postpone the delivery. When the lady at the end of the telephone asked why and she explained about the freezer and told her about Haatchi, the stranger was touched and asked to see a photograph of the three-legged dog they were rescuing.

An hour later, Colleen and Will received a call from Suzanne Brock, sister of company director David Brock, who told them they'd like to sponsor Haatchi and give him free food for life. Colleen couldn't believe it; she was so shocked she burst into tears. It was an incredibly generous gesture.

Little did they know then just how much Haatchi's story would touch people in ways they could never have imagined and lead to so many future acts of kindness.

Because she had found Haatchi via Facebook, Colleen had decided it was only right to set up a special page for him. For his first few entries, and describing the day that Colleen first met him, Haatchi 'wrote': '*Feb 14 – Happy Valentine's Day! It is even more special for me as today I secured my forever home! Bring on the love!*' He described himself as a '*comedian, entertainer and self-employed psychologist*'. Under 'Education' he said he studied surviving being hit by a train after being deliberately tied to the track at the '*University of life and hard knocks*'. On the dateline for February, he wrote: '*Left job at RSPCA – survival specialist*', adding that he took '*a crash course in the diversity of the human race, ranging from people determined to murder me, people who fought to keep me alive, through to people who want to enrich my life both physically and mentally for ever.*'

Colleen later posted photographs of his first walk (with Owen head down in his wheelchair as usual), as well as his first visit to the groomer, and even some video footage of him snoring as he slept. He was snapped raising money for Help for Heroes outside a superstore and within what seemed like days Haatchi had more than a thousand followers.

As more and more people came to learn of his story and were moved by it, pictures and videos of him started being shared around the world. To meet the demand for

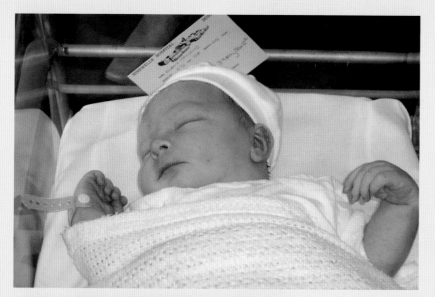

ABOVE Owen as a newborn in hospital.

LEFT Owen with his mother Kim.

BELOW Aged five on holiday with Nana Sara and Granddad Hugh.

ABOVE Haatchi's first night at Dogs and Kisses.   **BELOW** Haatchi and his new little buddy.

Who says
size matters?

ABOVE Owen in typical pose on Haatchi's first walk.

BELOW Owen and Haatchi test drive his new wheels in the snow.

LEFT Haatchi's portrait by Sara Abbott.

BELOW Haatchi helps with Little B's homework.

BOTTOM Haatchi relaxing into his early fundraising role.

ABOVE Did someone say dinner?   **BELOW** We're celebrities, get us out of here.

Inseparable buddies.

Haatchi teaching
Owen doga.

LEFT Corporal Howkins and his best buddy.

ABOVE Bedtime for Little B and his furry friends.

BELOW Goodnight huggles for the sleep bugs.

more, Colleen began posting new events like 'Kiss a Freckle Friday', with weekly close-up photos of Haatchi's freckly nose; and 'Throwback Thursday', a Facebook trend for old pictures. Owen began to feature in more of the shots as 'Me and my Little B' and looked delighted to have his big brave buddy to 'huggle'.

Colleen had also signed up to a Facebook page dedicated to raw feeding for dogs and picked up a few extra friends for Haatchi there too, including a lady named Jan Wolfe who managed some self-catering holiday cottages near Oban on the west coast of Scotland. Like Will and Colleen, she firmly believed that raw food helped to keep dogs in the optimum health. This was of special concern because of Haatchi's injuries.

The couple had already taken him to their local vet and asked him to assess his wounds. They were particularly worried about his tail, which was still bleeding. Through his frequent falls, he was damaging it further, so it had to be bandaged permanently. The vet warned them that if it became badly infected they might have to put Haatchi to sleep because the amputation had been done so close to his spine. From that day on, they knew they had to keep a watchful eye on him – just as they were accustomed to doing with Owen. As they put it, 'this had to work', so for the next few weeks they virtually followed Haatchi around the house hoping to catch him if he fell.

They also treated his leg stump every day, cleaning it up and applying aloe vera gel, and within a few weeks it began to heal. He never licked at it and didn't need a collar – it was as if he knew better.

Will and Colleen were beginning to realize how much would be involved in keeping Haatchi fit and healthy. He would need constant monitoring and frequent visits to the vet, all to be fitted in alongside Owen's schooling and medical appointments, plus the pressures of both of them working full-time. It was a sacrifice they were prepared to make, though, just to have the handsome Anatolian Shepherd in their lives.

What they hadn't expected, though, was the change Haatchi brought about in Little B. Suddenly he was so much happier. It was a surprise to everyone.

Owen had become increasingly tricky about taking his medicines, which he ingested mostly in liquid form via a syringe. He had told his father that he hated the taste. He had also started to have almost daily run-ins with Will and Colleen about eating healthy foods – especially green vegetables, which they wanted him to eat in order to boost his immune system and help ward off infections. But when he saw how good Haatchi was at eating his raw food and taking all his pills, Owen decided that he would be as brave as his dog.

Watched by his new best buddy, Little B would now line up all his medicines on the table in front of him in a specific order and make sure he got the worst-tasting ones over with first. He'd tell Haatchi and his father, 'I have to man up!' and then he'd drink them all down. It even got to the point that if his dad forgot to give him his medicine or was late, then Owen would remind him.

Haatchi also became invaluable for moral support whenever Little B had to go through any painful physiotherapy sessions, remaining at his side and showing his concern with a comforting lick from his big pink tongue. When he was very excited he'd speak to Owen in his special dog talk that made him sound a bit like Scooby-Doo. And, of course, there were always goodnight huggles before they both went to sleep.

Haatchi responded equally strongly to the child he now saw it as his duty to protect. When Owen went back to school the Monday after the rescue dog had come into their lives, Haatchi wandered restlessly around the house looking for his little boy and didn't settle until he came home. It was clear that he was missing his new best friend.

The following day, when Will went to fetch Owen from school, Haatchi sat in the window, his face pressed against the glass (making what the family dubbed 'nose art') until they returned. On day three, he took up his position at the window ten minutes before Will even left to collect Little B – and he has done that ever since. Just like Hachi, his Japanese namesake, he was watching and waiting for his owner to return.

In the first few days after Haatchi moved in with them, Will took Owen and the dogs out for their daily walk. As usual, his son adopted his default position – beanie hat on, head down, hands thrust into pockets, his body curled in on itself. The family even has a photograph of him in just that pose, with a bemused Haatchi looking on and wondering where his little buddy has gone.

One by one, strangers began to notice the unusual dog at their side. Delighted by his size and the fact that he seemed to be coping so well with three legs, they'd approach the group unabashed to say hello or stroke him, completely ignoring Owen.

Within two weeks of Haatchi's arrival, Little B shocked his father by asking if they could go out for a walk in the snow. Will happily agreed and they set off with Haatchi's lead tied loosely to the back of Owen's wheelchair. People still stared at the unusual family group, but now it was for a different reason. They were admiring the handsome three-legged dog and no longer focusing on the shy little boy in the wheelchair. Once again, complete strangers approached and asked about Haatchi. To Will's amazement, and before he could even respond, Owen unexpectedly lifted his head and told them the whole story, engaging with outsiders for the first time. Invariably, he'd make them cry with pity – especially women, whom Owen seemed to affect particularly. Will was astounded. 'It was an incredible transformation. He went from being painfully shy to working the crowd!'

The story of how Haatchi lost his leg and tail seemed to affect people differently. The older they were, and the more passionately they felt about animals, the more profoundly it upset them. Some were reduced to tears in the street, especially when they heard that his injuries were as a result of cruelty.

Colleen and Will were careful to keep the full horror of what had happened to him from small children, so they told Owen just to say that he'd been hit by a train and then they warned kids about the dangers of playing near railway tracks. Young and old were fascinated by how well Haatchi managed with only three legs, and would almost always tell Owen what a 'cool' dog he had before complimenting him on his 'wheels'.

Whatever the age of his audience, Owen soon learned how to tug at their heartstrings and seemed to enjoy being the narrator of his 'awesome' dog's incredible survival story.

Everyone in the family, from Kim to Owen's grandparents, noticed the difference in him almost straight away. Many of them had been worried about Will and Colleen taking on a disabled dog on top of everything else, but they were soon won over as Owen began to blossom in Haatchi's company. Kim said: 'At first I thought, "Oh no, not another dog!" but then I saw how Owen started to change and grow more confident. All he talked about was Haatchi this and Haatchi that. He really came into his own. That dog has been like a miracle.'

For the first time in his young life Owen realized that people weren't interested in him or staring at him because he was different but because he had a 'cool' dog. Before too long he asked Will to bring Haatchi with him when he collected him from school so that his friends could meet him, and he soon made his unusual pet the subject of projects and artworks.

His teachers had already commented on the difference in Owen in class. Instead of asking people to reach for something or pick an item up if he dropped it, he had begun trying to do it for himself. He even started to admit to liking a few of the girls in his class – all of whom had fallen for Haatchi, of course – and asked Colleen to write a letter to one of them for him.

It was as if Little B had discovered his own independence through watching Haatchi find his.

His scholastic abilities improved dramatically too, especially in literacy and maths, and he went from below average to average or above in a matter of months. Staff and family alike were equally impressed. With Haatchi at his side, Owen started knuckling down to his homework at night and would open his laptop by himself to start on his 'mathletics' – explaining everything to his dog, who sat next to him on the sofa, cocking his head as if taking it all in.

Then one day Little B did something that neither his family nor his teachers would ever have thought he'd do. He stood up in front of a class of younger children and spoke of his ambition to learn to walk again. He announced that he was going to do it with the help of his special dog. There wasn't a dry eye in the house.

Everyone who witnessed the change in Owen accepted that it was largely down to Haatchi. The dog had given him a newfound level of confidence that he probably couldn't have got from another human. They acted like a team and they worked together to get through their days.

Through his raw animal love and acceptance, Haatchi had taught Owen the true meaning of friendship.

Less than a month after Haatchi's arrival, Will and Colleen decided to take him and Little B to the famous Crufts dog show at the National Exhibition Centre in Birmingham. Their sponsors, Natural Instinct, had booked a stand there to promote their wares, so the couple offered to go and support them in return for their kindness. They also wanted to take Haatchi along to show people that, although he'd started off in a very fragile state, he was now incredibly healthy and getting better by the day, which they felt spoke volumes for his raw-food diet.

The visit to the NEC would be the biggest public outing Owen had ever been on, with several thousand people in attendance. Within hours of their arrival it was obvious to everyone that Haatchi was a massive crowd-pleaser. Just one look at him would stop people in their tracks. At various times, his new fans would be seven deep around the stand. Losing any shyness they might previously have had, complete strangers would drop to their knees to hug him or even start rolling about with him on the floor.

Neither Will nor Colleen had had any idea that he would have that kind of effect, and they were staggered to see how well the public responded to him.

With show-goers flocking to the little raw-food stand, Owen suddenly had a full-time job explaining to them all what had happened to Haatchi. He soon became as sought after as his dog, as he talked to everyone and happily posed for photographs with his new buddy. He even gave some media interviews. Watching him perform, Will and Colleen could hardly believe this was the same little boy who had previously barely said a word to anyone in public.

'That was the day it all began,' Colleen remembered. 'It was as if Little B had been a bud waiting for the light and love of Haatchi to make him flower. Up until that moment, he was in the world, but he was not of the world. Only a tiny part of him was visible and known to anybody. Haatchi made it possible for the whole world to know what a beautiful and remarkable little boy Owen Howkins really is.'

There were several other pleasant surprises that day too. Suzanne Syers from UKGSR, who'd helped organize Haatchi's eleventh-hour 'rescue' from Harmsworth Hospital, dropped by to see them on their stand. She was delighted finally to meet the big tri-paw dog she'd helped save, and his new family was thrilled to be able to thank her in person.

On a stand opposite theirs at Crufts was a canine masseur named Joanne Cleeve, who had recently set up her own business, K9 Rehabilitation, based in Oxfordshire. She wandered over to meet Haatchi and immediately fell for the dog with the amber eyes. She asked if she could massage him and Haatchi responded like a regular to her healing hands. Before they knew it, Will and Colleen were being offered free or discounted massages for Haatchi whenever they turned up at one of the dog shows she attended, just to show people how much it helped him.

Haatchi had another surprise visitor – Ross McCarthy from Dogs and Kisses, who'd kindly taken him in. The pair were clearly delighted to be reunited, as Ross dropped to his knees and Haatchi lay semi-comatose, snoring gently in his lap.

Back home after Crufts, Haatchi was still learning how to manage with a missing leg. Having just three was starting to take a toll on his remaining paws. He had a little leather boot made for his rear paw to give it extra tread, which especially assisted him when he tried to stand up. Will and Colleen had installed laminated wood flooring for Owen, because it gave him greater manoeuvrability in his walking frame and wheelchair and also because carpet exacerbated his breathing problems. But polished floors were not ideal for a growing tri-paw.

Ever the survivor, though, it didn't take Haatchi long to get the hang of his new condition and of his environment, and he adjusted remarkably well. He even figured out how to get his enormous frame through the small dogflap the couple had installed in the back door for Mr Pixel. Colleen grabbed her camera and managed to film the Anatolian Shepherd as his head and shoulders burst through (sending the plastic flap flying). Then he gingerly put first one leg and then the other through before somehow sliding the rest of his huge body after it. They couldn't believe what they'd just witnessed.

Ingenious as he might be, he was still a large, heavy dog (and getting bigger by the week) and his spine started to twist as he positioned his rear leg more to the middle and turned it out for better support. At the recommendation of their vet, Will and Colleen took him to Greyfriars Veterinary Rehabilitation and Hydrotherapy Centre in Guildford, where staff heard his story of survival and kindly offered to help out. They halved the fees for the hydrotherapy sessions he'd need twice a week and within a month he was swimming unaided, holding his balance on his own for the first time as his core muscles built up.

'There is something about Haatchi that makes people do wonderful things,' Colleen said. 'Everyone wants to make it up to him for what happened. Having witnessed the worst of humanity, he seems to bring out the best.'

She continued to post news of his progress on Facebook, where he was still accumulating hundreds of new followers as his incredible story went viral. He began to be featured in local and national media, which only opened even more doors. Gifts and treats started arriving for him and Little B in the mail.

Owen had always loved receiving postcards – ever since Colleen's mother, Kathryn, sent him one all the way from New Zealand – so he was very excited to get even more from his and Haatchi's many fans around the globe. One American family, from Idaho, sent him a fabric map of the world, so Will created a padded 'postcard map' out of it to hang on Owen's wall and mark off each new country. The UK and Europe quickly filled up with coloured pins, so the more exotic the postmark, the better. Will even set up a special PO box for Owen so that their postman wouldn't be inundated.

There were more kind gestures when a canine chiropractor named Jenny Lewis got in touch with the family and offered to give Haatchi treatments using the McTimoney chiropractic treatment. He completely relaxed during the procedure and Will and Colleen were amazed to watch his eyes close in bliss each time Jenny manipulated the tight joints in his spine.

Owen, meanwhile, was enjoying someone else getting all the medical attention in the family for a change – even though he was having his own problems as his physical condition deteriorated.

Mentally and emotionally he was very much better, but his breathing issues weren't improving and he was developing a nasty acid reflux problem. Fortunately, he had Haatchi to distract him.

Touched by the generosity of all those who had offered to help their latest rescue dog, Will and Colleen started to attend other dog shows with him and Little B in support of their many new friends and sponsors. Over the course of the next few months, they went to events such as Bark in the Park in Basingstoke, Discover Dogs at Earls Court, Paws in the Park in Maidstone, the Egham Royal County Show, and many other charity shows, including of course the Royal Air Force Family Day at RAF Odiham. Each outing proved to be great fun, with Haatchi and Owen getting lots of attention and the Anatolian Shepherd winning all sorts of prizes for anything from 'Best Rescue' to 'Best Friend'.

Owen loved showing him off and their outings together were especially good for teaching both boy and dog how to socialize. And it wasn't just Little B who appeared to benefit from Haatchi's presence. Will and Colleen also noticed a big change in the way other people looked at or even spoke to Owen. It was as if having a disabled dog at his side made him somehow more approachable.

During the summer of the 2012 London Olympics, Will took three weeks off work to stay at home with Owen so that they could watch it on TV every day. Little B was even allowed to stay up for the opening ceremony, his arm around Haatchi's neck throughout.

Then the Paralympics began and Will noticed how fascinated and impressed his son was by all those who had overcome their disabilities to become inspirational sportsmen and women. Through the Tickets for Troops website, he managed to get them seats at a few of the events. They took Will's six-year-old niece Molly along with Owen to watch a round of bocce (which is like boules or petanque but played with soft balls). Little B loved those games and was completely gripped by the whole event. Will believed it taught him a great deal about being independent and becoming his own man regardless of the fact that he was in a wheelchair. The family felt it was also good for Molly to be in that environment and see just how normal disabled people's lives can be.

In August, Haatchi was awarded the accolade of Top

Dog in Drontal's Give Your Dog A Bone competition. The panel of judges chose him from hundreds of entries because, they said, he 'stood out', and they added, 'The remarkable story behind Haatchi's survival and the equally remarkable family into which he has been adopted are a shining example of the special bond dogs share with their owners.'

The family decided to donate their prizes, which included a camcorder and a holiday voucher worth £1,000, to the Make A Wish Foundation for seriously ill children and they were auctioned at a charity event at the Dorchester Hotel in London.

At the Pup Aid event in Primrose Hill, London – set up to raise awareness about the horrific practices of puppy farming – Haatchi won Best in Show and his prize this time was a painting by Sara Abbott, a renowned pet portrait artist. Usually Sara offers show prizewinners a 60cm square head-and-shoulders portrait, but when she met the dog who'd already grown to the size of a Shetland pony she knew she had to think on a much grander scale. She decided straight away that this painting had to be of his whole body, because the power behind Haatchi's story was his missing leg. Sara has painted hundreds of dogs in her career, but, like so many other people, she felt she had never met one quite like Haatchi. 'It is as if he is a human in a dog's body,' she said. 'He just seems to understand everything.'

Sara visited the family home and took scores of photographs to work from, but it was when Haatchi heard

Owen's voice off to one side of the garden and turned to look at him that she got the shot on which she based the final metre-square painting. When it was finished the family travelled to her home in Brighton for the grand unveiling – accompanied by TV vet Marc Abraham (who organized Pup Aid) – and both Owen and Colleen burst into tears when they saw what Sara had done. *Watching Owen* now hangs in pride of place in the Howkins family's living room, and is admired by everyone who sees it. Haatchi and Little B even had their own business cards printed featuring the portrait.

In September 2012, Owen was due to start at junior school in Basingstoke – a place that not only was wheelchair friendly but had been carefully selected to allow him to be treated normally and not in a specialist environment.

With none of his primary-school classmates moving with him and only the help of two special needs assistants, who'd take turns to do morning and afternoon shifts, everyone was very concerned about how the still sometimes shy little boy would respond in a strange new environment.

Keen to help Little B all she could, especially when it came to keeping up with his schoolmates, Colleen came up with a plan to raise money for a state-of-the-art electric wheelchair for him to use at his new school. The idea came to her in a dream. 'I was wheeling Owen around in his horrible NHS wheelchair but there was a coin slot in the arm. As we walked, people came up and put £1 coins into the slot. Each time they did, the wheelchair morphed into something better and better until it became a top-of-the-range electric one.'

Colleen woke up early the next morning and told Will she was going to do a £1 wheelchair walk to raise the £8,000–£12,000 they would need for the new chair, depending on its specification. She figured that if all their friends (and Haatchi's followers on Facebook) donated £1, they could at least raise enough for the deposit. Her aim was to walk from Southampton Hospital to their home town of Basingstoke, a distance of thirty-one miles, in a day.

Thanks to the surprise generosity of colleagues, Colleen and Will were given a huge boost with the news of a £5,000 grant towards the cost of the new wheelchair. Then, when Colleen set up a new events page on Facebook for the charity walk, they were swamped with donations. She'd asked everyone to donate £1, but some people sent in up to £300 at a time and from as far away as America. To begin with she thought she must have written the wrong figure, so she contacted all the donors individually to tell them she was only asking for £1 each. Every single one of them told her that they'd understood perfectly but wanted them to have the extra money anyway. She was amazed.

The walk was planned for December 2012 and the couple raised the extra £3,000 they needed just in time. Then the wheelchair company informed them that they would be VAT-exempt because Owen was registered disabled, which meant that the price they thought they would have to pay unexpectedly dropped by 20 per cent. Armed with this information, Colleen made an immediate announcement on Facebook asking people to stop sending money, but many of their followers were so impressed by their honesty that they kept donating anyway.

In the end, Colleen and Will gave the surplus £1,068 they'd raised to the Starlight children's charity, which offers days out and gifts for terminally ill children and their families.

In preparation for the walk, Colleen and Will had T-shirts made up which read: 'Never Walk Alone'. The back said: 'It's Not How Many Legs or Wheels. It's Who Journeys With You'.

A new friend agreed to make a batch of special Haatchi cakepops featuring his face for them to eat and give away en route, but at the last minute she refused to charge them for them because she'd unexpectedly won £500 in a charity draw and said she believed her good fortune was 'Haatchi karma'.

Colleen was accompanied on her walk by two friends, Laura Edmonston and Max Rafferty – the boyfriend of one of her closest friends, Lisa Ford. Will, Haatchi and Little B joined them periodically for moral support. Other friends, their children and dogs, cheered them along their route. Donors, meanwhile, could follow their progress on Facebook and on YouTube, and by the time the walk ended – with heavy feet but light hearts – Haatchi and

Little B were waiting for Colleen and her friends at Basingstoke Hospital.

Owen's brand-new wheelchair was unveiled to him as a surprise during a routine visit to collect Haatchi's raw food from the Natural Instinct shop. Will filmed the moment when his son was invited to pull off the white sheet covering the chair and he managed to get close-ups of Little B gasping at the sight of his stunning new wheels.

Painted electric blue and with four-wheel drive so it could go off road, the state-of-the-art machine had lights and indicators as well as a roll-bar, horn, racing seatbelts and a personalized number plate spelling the name Owen.

After his first spin around the block (Haatchi ever at his side), Little B grinned and gave his new chair the thumbs-up. 'Totally awesome!' he decreed.

His family all hoped it would give him the boost he needed as he settled into his new school and what would undoubtedly be a scary new phase in his life.

5

*'He is your friend, your partner, your defender, your dog. You are
his life, his love, his leader. He will be yours, faithful and true, to
the last beat of his heart. You owe it to him to be worthy of such
devotion.'*

Unknown

O
N LITTLE B'S FIRST day at his new school, Will and
Colleen took Haatchi along in the back of the car so
that Owen could show him off. The sight of the furry tri-
paw dog attracted a lot of excitable interest, which the
family was only too happy to capitalize on.

Owen's new school chums were at the perfect age to
learn about both disability and animal welfare, and
Colleen was especially impressed by their reaction to
Haatchi as he wiggled his body and spoke to them in pure
Scooby-Doo. She had always known that she wanted to
train Haatchi as a therapy dog and the more she saw of
how people responded to him, the more determined she
became to take him down that path.

The couple left Owen in the care of his new teacher, hoping for the best. When he eventually came home from school later that day, though, he was crying and they were naturally concerned. Fearing someone might have picked on his son, Will asked him what was wrong as he buried his face in Haatchi's neck.

'I don't like all the girls calling me cute!' Little B sobbed.

Will and Colleen tried not to laugh.

They soon discovered that when the girls at school told Little B he was cute, he thought they were referring to the fact that he was little. It took a week to calm him down and Will had to explain that cute wasn't anything bad at all.

'I only wish the girls at my school had thought I was cuteness personified!' he insisted.

Within a short space of time Owen was loving his new school – not least because he had staff and fellow pupils eating out of his hand. Discovering his own wicked sense of humour, he developed a cheeky way about him and soon made a circle of friends who became fiercely protective of him.

Like his dad, he enjoyed all things technological and did especially well at maths, literacy and art, as well as reading and French. Both in and out of the classroom he developed a strong friendship base and everyone seemed eager to support him.

His two special needs assistants, Miss O'Hagan and Mrs Hayward – whose job-share costs were split between the school and the local authority – took turns to help him do the things he couldn't, such as using the toilet or reaching something beyond his range. Will had warned them not to let Owen take advantage, as it was important that he continued to learn how to be independent.

Having gone to a Church of England school himself, Will had initially been keen for Owen to attend one as well, but the nearest one to them wasn't especially wheel-chair friendly and would have been 'a logistical nightmare' for Owen. His new school was much more suitable, and from the outset the staff couldn't do enough for Owen. Within days, his family knew that they'd made the right decision. They had always emphasized that Owen was completely normal apart from his muscle spasms, and it was important to them that he was treated just like any other little boy. He had someone to help with the problems that were specific to him, and – with his new wheels – he was capable of keeping up with the rest of his class.

And just like any little boy, he had to be reminded to behave, do his homework, eat his vegetables and not stay up too late on school nights playing his computer games.

Even sweet-natured Haatchi had to be reprimanded occasionally. Although he loved people and was good with strangers, behaving well even at busy shows, his Anatolian guard-dog ancestry meant that he had taken to barking at anyone who walked past the house – especially whenever he was pressing his nose against the window waiting for Owen. His instinct was to protect his family and so he would also bark at any dog – especially a nervous or aggressive one – that he perceived as a threat. As his bark was like a foghorn, it was usually enough to frighten them (and their owners) away.

Colleen was worried about his barking at first, but then a breeder of Anatolian Shepherds whom they had met at Crufts reassured her. She told her that all the favourable publicity Haatchi was getting could only be good for the breed, which was at risk of being put on to a dangerous dogs list by the authorities because of its guardian tendencies. She hoped that Haatchi's famously mellow nature might single-handedly save Anatolian Shepherds from being misunderstood.

The calm way he generally behaved around people (other than those walking past his window) convinced Will and Colleen that, although nobody had ever come forward to claim a missing Anatolian Shepherd, Haatchi must have experienced love and affection at some point in his young life. The fact that he seemed to know about human kindness led Colleen to believe he must have spent his early weeks in a place where he was loved – especially by children, to whom he always responded so well. She suspected something then happened – maybe he grew too big or became too boisterous or expensive – and he was given away or stolen. Sadly, he ended up with the man who took him to the railway tracks and treated him so cruelly. She and Will refused to harbour vengeful thoughts, however. 'I believe in karma,' said Colleen, 'and having Haatchi has only reinforced that view. Good things seem to happen to everyone who helps him, including us. I only hope that whoever did this to him sees how many people's lives have been changed by him for the better. The dog that man tried to kill is having the most wonderful life and bringing joy and comfort to others, especially to Little B. He may have planned to extinguish that life but his plan totally backfired.'

Thanks to Haatchi's sunny attitude, the family focused only on the positives. As they were quick to point out, if he hadn't been treated so cruelly in the first place then he and Owen would never have met and rescued each other. Now, thanks to him, they've been able to advance global awareness and understanding about Owen's rare syndrome, as well as about disability and animal welfare in general. To them the difference Haatchi has made to Owen's life has been nothing short of a miracle, and rather than taking it for granted or keeping it to themselves, they have tried hard to make that same feel-good factor available to others by getting involved in a great many charity events – for Owen's sake too – and by training Haatchi as a Pets as a therapy dog.

Haatchi's training as one of the UK's five thousand Pets As Therapy (PAT) dogs began when he was only a few months old. After he had passed the health, temperament and suitability assessment, Colleen taught him some basic commands, such as 'Sit' and how to take a treat politely. He was a natural at both. Then she set off a series of loud noises near him – including popping balloons, dropping heavy objects and ringing bells – to make sure he reacted calmly. He never made a fuss and responded in his usual laid-back way.

Thanks to their frequent visits to various charity events and dog shows, plus his growing numbers of followers on Facebook and Twitter, the family began to receive requests for Haatchi to visit the sick or injured. One lady who approached them at Crufts was very poorly and lying prone in a wheelchair, but when she saw Haatchi at the show her smile 'could have lit up London'.

Another admirer was a little girl in Southampton, who fell in love with Haatchi when she met him at a dog show and began to follow him on Facebook. Later, Colleen found out that she was going into hospital for major surgery so she asked the girl's parents if it might cheer her up if Haatchi went to visit her. They readily agreed.

Officially, Haatchi had yet to be registered as a PAT dog before he could enter hospitals and care homes, for reasons of public liability insurance. The system makes sure to match the right dog to the right location and patient, depending on the animal's size and temperament. Keen to lift the sick girl's spirits, though, Colleen drove Haatchi to the hospital where she was an in-patient in the hope that she might at least be able to see him from the window of her ward. As they stood outside the entrance of the hospital, the doorway quickly became blocked with people wanting to pet him and say hello. The sister on the little girl's ward looked out of the window, saw what was happening and told the girl's father that Colleen could bring Haatchi up. She took a deep breath and told Haatchi, 'Okay, buddy, let's see how you cope with this!' Inside, the floors were very shiny but he managed to walk on them, and when he got to the ward he went straight to the girl's cubicle and quietly nuzzled her hand, just as he had when he first met Owen. It was all her parents could do to stop her jumping out of bed to throw her arms around his neck.

Colleen gave the little girl a butterfly necklace and some perfume, and within a few days they heard from her parents that she had made a good enough recovery to go home for a while. All the other children on the ward wanted to see Haatchi as well, including one little boy who could barely lift his head but still smiled broadly when he spotted the three-legged dog.

The experience was intensely moving for Colleen, who said that up until that day she'd had a 'fairytale' vision of children improving just from seeing Haatchi. The reality was that, for some of them, nothing could help. Interestingly, although almost all of the children were pleased to meet him, the ones who appeared to be most affected by him were their parents, as if he gave them a five-minute holiday from worrying about their children. Haatchi also proved to be a welcome distraction for the staff, even for one nurse who'd previously been terrified of dogs.

Having witnessed how much joy he spread, Colleen and Will continued to visit anyone in the Greater London area who might benefit from Haatchi's presence. He was especially good at lifting the spirits of the elderly and those suffering from anxiety or depression. Between them, they quietly brought smiles to the faces of scores of people.

At another establishment, Haatchi had a dramatic effect on a nine-year-old boy with attention deficit disorder (ADD). The boy's eyes constantly darted left and right and he couldn't sit still, but he took one look at Haatchi and calmed down so dramatically that his mother burst into tears because she hadn't seen him so contented in years.

Will was especially keen for him to work with veterans who had been injured in action; having served in Afghanistan and Iraq, several colleagues of his were wounded. Although he had always been aware that pet-assisted therapy was supposed to help injured service personnel to convalesce, in the past he had been a little sceptical, but having seen Haatchi's effect on Owen he realized there really was something in it.

Will thought that the dog could be particularly therapeutic to those who'd lost limbs in action. Having met a few amputees at charity events and dog shows – including one who thanked them for keeping Haatchi alive before lifting his trousers and proudly showing them his fake leg – Will and Colleen had seen how well they responded to the big three-legged dog. Their dream was to be able to take him to Headley Court in Surrey and the Help for Heroes facility at Tedworth House in Wiltshire – two of Britain's leading rehabilitation hospitals.

Until that time, Haatchi had been a regular and welcome visitor at a local hospice and at a hospital not far from home. On one visit, he limped up to a soldier with only one arm left of all his limbs, and plopped himself down right next to him. Staff reported later that the man had been very depressed but he was overcome to meet what Colleen and Will describe as 'our furry cuddle monster' and within a few minutes of seeing how well Haatchi coped with three legs, he was beside himself with joy.

News of Haatchi's story and the effect he was having on people quickly spread, and in October 2012 he was nominated for a special award from the International Fund for Animal Welfare (IFAW), one of the largest animal welfare charities in the world. The person who nominated him was Jez Rose, a behaviour expert and motivational speaker, who had worked with Colleen at a seminar and was deeply moved by Haatchi's tale. Robbie Marsland, the UK director of IFAW, said, 'When we heard Haatchi's amazing story of survival and the very special relationship he has with Owen, we knew he had to be our IFAW Animal of the Year.'

The presentation was made at the House of Lords at the Animal Action Awards hosted by Baroness Gale. Haatchi received his trophy from Brian May, the lead guitarist with the band Queen, who has become as famous for his concerns about animal welfare as he is as a rock star. Colleen thought he was wonderful with both Haatchi and Owen, who acted as if he met a rock legend every day. The family was given superstar treatment, and Little B was on top of the world. He sat at the head of the table and everybody came to talk to him, including the Lord Speaker, and TV personality and birdwatcher Bill Oddie. The press took photographs on the Riverside Terrace afterwards and

Owen held his glass trophy aloft. It was a day the family will never forget.

Back home, Haatchi's incredible recovery continued to confound his vet and all the gloomy predictions of how he would cope without a leg. Within a year of being rescued, he had become so agile on three legs that he could keep up with Mr Pixel and Colleen's other dogs on a run. In peak condition, and with his long stride and barrel chest, it seemed there was nothing Haatchi couldn't do.

The family was booked to go back to Crufts in March to support their friends and sponsors and they were especially delighted when Haatchi was nominated for the coveted Friends for Life Award, to be decided by a public vote. Having been picked for the final from more than twenty thousand dogs, Haatchi was up against four other pets, all of them selected for their devotion to their owners or for their outstanding bravery. Among them was Brin, an abandoned Afghani stray, who had barked to alert two soldiers to a roadside bomb that would have killed them, and then survived being captured by the Taliban. There was also Janus, a Belgian Malinois, who had made more than four hundred arrests as a police dog in the West Midlands. Daisy, a Bull Mastiff, had helped a family recover from the loss of their six-year-old son; and Max and Ziggy – two assistance dogs – had helped their owners find love.

Owen was delighted that his dog had been nominated and even more excited when – because they had been brought to public attention – he and Haatchi were invited to appear on *This Morning* with Holly Willoughby and Phillip Schofield as part of a national Rare Disease Day.

Head high and with his inscrutable smile, Owen told the cameras: 'I used to be scared of strangers, then Haatchi came along and now I'm not. I didn't really meet many others with disabilities and felt like the odd one out, which made me really sad. But then I saw Haatchi and I saw how strong he was, even though he only had three legs. I became stronger myself. I love him so much.' Holly and Phillip were clearly smitten and wished him all the best for Crufts.

The organizers of the famous dog show created short films featuring each of the finalists so that the public could choose which one they wanted to win via telephone voting lines. Owen sat on the sofa next to his special dog, hugged him and introduced 'my best friend Haatchi'.

The nation melted.

The Duchess of York later sent a toy Buckingham Palace Corgi, and scores of other well-wishers sent cards and toys, treats and sweets.

And then disaster struck. A month before the family was due to go to Crufts to find out how many people had voted for Haatchi, he playfully chased Mr Pixel out of the house through the giant dogflap on a frosty February night. Out in the garden, he slipped on some black ice. Will and Colleen heard a huge bang and then a tiny whimper. They rushed out to find Haatchi lying on the ground looking up at them pitifully. Colleen feared at first that he might have broken his back.

The couple helped the massive dog inside, wrapped him in towels and laid him on his big padded bed with his favourite fluffy toy, Harold Hedgehog (a gift from a well-wisher and the only one he hadn't ripped apart). Haatchi barely moved for two days and Colleen and Will posted online that he had what they called an 'ouch ouch'. The vet who saw him first said that he must have done the splits, because he had torn his abductor, stomach and pectoral muscles. He had also damaged his back leg and strained his front ones. Ouch ouch indeed.

Owen lay on Haatchi's bed and hugged his injured friend whenever he could. Will and Colleen often caught them having private whispered conversations that Little B made clear were strictly between a boy and his dog. He knew what it was like to feel pain – he'd known it all his life – and just as the two of them had always accepted each other's differences, now they were a team working together to overcome the problems they each faced.

Even after the swelling in Haatchi's torn muscles went down, the family was warned it would take several weeks for him to recover. At a time when they were saving hard for their wedding that August, Will and Colleen were told he'd need expensive hydrotherapy and other treatments. He could have no outside walks at all to begin with, and then only limited exercise for several weeks, if not months. His home would basically become an oversized kennel, which meant that they were right back to square one with him from the previous year.

In spite of his cheery disposition, Haatchi became

visibly depressed at being confined to the house. He would give 'the howl of all howls' whenever Will or Colleen went out for a walk with Mr Pixel or the other dogs and would sit in the window crying. It was heartbreaking for all concerned.

Using a harness they had bought to help lift him to his feet and support his weight, Will eventually let him potter on the front lawn on a lead, which boosted his morale enormously. Then, as his injuries slowly began to heal, he was allowed as far as the next house to sniff their grass, and then the next, and so on.

The couple took him back for some hydrotherapy sessions and he also had ultrasound treatment and acupuncture with therapist Susanna Alwen. Whenever her needles hit the right spot, Haatchi would go into a kind of trance – lying still and calm, swaying slightly, with a faraway look in his eyes, as if he was the most relaxed, pain-free dog in the world. Colleen took a photograph of him lying on Susanna's special mat, needles sticking out all over him, with what she describes as an 'Om' expression of distracted bliss. After his first session of acupuncture, he slept for five hours straight and when he woke up his attitude was, 'Yay! I'm all better!'

'Speaking' to them in his special doggy language, he was virtually smiling for the camera and – although he still faced a great deal of rehabilitation – he was once again the dog they knew and loved.

Haatchi wasn't out of the woods yet, by any means, but he was well enough to go to Crufts in March with Owen and meet many more of his devoted fans, including Jan Wolfe, the lady who'd befriended Colleen on Facebook over their shared interest in raw food for dogs.

There were other nice surprises too. A company called OrthoPets Europe who saw Haatchi with Owen at Crufts gave him one of their special 'Help 'Em Up' harnesses with a handle, which made it easier to lift him to his feet than the one he already had, and would also give him greater support when his back leg tired. The managing director of OrthoPets, Rod Hunt, fell in love with Haatchi's story and said it was the least the company could do: they could see that if anything happened to that dog, then Owen's life would quickly degenerate too. (Haatchi adapted well to the new harness and, before long, became excited every time he saw it because it meant he'd be going for a walk.)

Having spent the final day of the show being patted and hugged in between posing with Little B for photographs, it was time for Haatchi and his proud family to await the formal announcement of which dog had won the Friends for Life Award. All five finalists and their owners were invited into the main arena. Will and Colleen helped Haatchi and Owen take their place in the spotlight as TV presenter Clare Balding stepped forward to introduce the award. The short films for each nominee were shown, and then they were each interviewed live for the BBC.

'Haatchi made me more confident,' Owen said softly into the microphone as the TV lights dazzled him. Then he clammed up completely, giving everyone a glimpse of the shy little boy he had once been.

John Spurling, vice president of the Kennel Club, took the microphone as the house lights were dimmed, opened a special envelope and announced, 'The winner of Friends for Life, with fifty-four per cent of the vote, is – Owen and Haatchi!'

A huge cheer went up from the crowd. Owen's face broke into an enormous grin, and an emotional Will leaned forward to hug and kiss his son. They were presented with a large engraved crystal vase and then the television crews lined up to interview Owen as he cradled the prize in his lap. With Haatchi sitting calmly at his side, the little boy – who would have been terrified of the limelight a year previously – lifted his head, beamed at the cameras, and said: 'It feels brilliant to win. I'm really happy I got this. I want to thank all of you for voting for me.' He added that Haatchi was 'the brilliantest dog in the world,' and said finally, 'I am more than happy. I am mega mega *mega* happy!'

The pair won £1,500 to give to the charity of their choice and they picked a children's hospice called Naomi House near their home in Hampshire. Owen was also presented with some Olympics badges because he'd so loved watching the Paralympics with his dad and announced that he'd like to be a Paralympian one day.

Ending what had been an incredible couple of days, Will proudly pushed Little B on a victory lap of the arena as he waved to the clapping crowd, the grin still fixed firmly to his face.

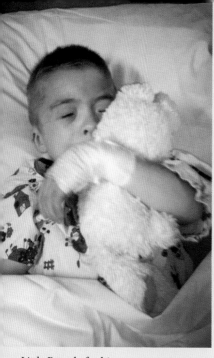

Little B ready for his next operation.

Veteran dog-show judge.

Time to read our postcards – I think we're going to need our own PO box, Dad!

ABOVE Proud stepmum Colleen.

RIGHT Now I'm a rock star!

LEFT Nigel Morris, the rail supervisor who was the first to find Haatchi.

Reunited with Siobhan, the RSPCA inspector who rescued Haatchi.

ABOVE On the *This Morning* sofa with Phillip and Holly.

BELOW Winning 'Friends for Life' at Crufts.

LEFT
Spreading
some Haatchi
love on
the water
treadmill.

BELOW
Anyone
fancy a dip?
With Angela
Griffiths
and Jessica
Blackman.

Sporting the
new harness.

ABOVE First day on my paws.

ABOVE Ouch Ouch operation.

ABOVE How many rock stars do you know? With Brian May.

BELOW Winners of the Braveheart Award with Rupert Grint.

The proud groom and his best man.

The happiest of endings.

The bride and groom with their best man and best dog.

6

*'There is no faith which has never yet been broken
except that of a truly faithful dog.'*

Konrad Lorenz

BY THE TIME Owen and Haatchi were featuring on news bulletins around the world thanks to Crufts, Corporal Will Howkins had come to a major decision.

Delighted as he was that his son had a whole new lease of life because of his amazing dog, it wasn't always easy to remain so positive in the face of Owen's deteriorating health. The muscle spasms and the effect they were having on his eyesight were definitely getting worse, as was his breathing. In constant pain, with blurred vision and poor balance, his care was becoming increasingly difficult to manage at school and at the childminder's where he stayed after school for a few hours a week.

No one could any longer say with certainty what Owen's long-term prognosis was, because in just a few years his condition had worsened markedly.

Colds and coughs had been a risk for him since birth and with one particularly bad infection Owen had to go to Southampton Hospital as an emergency case.

Even though Will had the love and support of Colleen as well as of his and Kim's families, he was becoming mentally and physically exhausted. Whenever Kim was in the country she was able to offer him respite periods by taking Owen for weekends or away on holiday. But she had been back to Afghanistan on a third tour and had also been sent elsewhere. Juggling his demanding full-time job with being the primary carer began to take its toll, especially when he needed to make up to six checks every night on Owen's oxygen supply.

Colleen began to worry that Will's broken sleep patterns might affect his work as a helicopter propulsion engineer. Servicemen's and women's lives depended on his getting things right, and he was never able to have a solid night's sleep; most days he was exhausted before he even got to his base and then he would be working on maybe eight helicopters at the same time. Colleen feared it was getting to the point where it was almost irresponsible to keep going.

Then there were the school runs, plus Owen's frequent medical appointments and visits to his dietician and or for yet another sleep study.

The RAF had been very accommodating about Will's unusual situation at home, but he was overdue for a foreign posting, with a possible trip to war-torn Syria looming. The couple was anxious about the possibility of him going somewhere so dangerous, and also wondered how they would manage Owen's needs with Colleen and Kim both working full-time.

Colleen soon came to believe that there was only one answer: Will would have to leave the RAF, even though she knew it would be a very hard decision for him to make. He was adamant that she shouldn't give up her job to care full-time for his son (even though she would have done so if that was what was required), so that was their only choice.

He could have tried to seek work elsewhere, but they couldn't imagine any other employer being as accommodating as the RAF had been, especially not in a straitened financial climate. Living on a single wage would be tough on them all, but Colleen also felt very strongly that Will needed to spend the next few years with his son. 'The bond between them is just beautiful,' she said, 'and none of us knows how long they've got together.'

When she first planted the seed about Will taking a career break to become Owen's full-time carer, he was resistant. He had joined the RAF as a teenager after being inspired by an uncle who was a squadron leader. He loved his job and the trade that he had learned along the way. He'd recently been promoted and hoped to attain the rank of sergeant one day. He'd served at home and abroad for Queen and country, and couldn't imagine being what he called 'a sponger', living on a carer's allowance.

Colleen and his family were quick to point out that not only had he earned the right to a break after fifteen years' loyal service in the armed forces, but that he'd be working jolly hard for every penny of any allowances to which he'd be entitled. She hoped he might even find time to pursue his passions for painting and golf, and finally to have some time to himself after what had been an intensely stressful six years since Little B was first diagnosed.

As Will agonized over what to do, in the end Colleen asked him, 'What do you really want?' He replied, 'I want to be with Owen.' She told him in that case he had his answer.

In December 2012, and with mixed feelings, Will took voluntary redundancy and left the RAF. He had a quiet beer with a few mates and then handed in his uniform. One of the first things he bought with some of his redundancy money was a new manual wheelchair for Owen – which was much more manageable indoors than his previous one – complete with solid wheels specially painted with Haatchi's face.

Little B was determined to contribute to the cost, so he asked his father to help him bake some cakes – painstakingly stirring the mixture and decorating the finished products in spite of his stiff hands – and then he held a cake sale at school, which raised more than £300.

When he was presented with his new chair in January, he was initially more interested in opening the present they'd bought for Haatchi first so that his best buddy didn't feel left out.

It took a while for Will to adjust to his new life as a stay-at-home dad, and he hated not being a breadwinner any more, but he wasn't someone to sit around doing nothing. Within months he'd been formally trained, vetted and appointed as a school's assistant to help out part-time in Owen's class. A natural with kids and someone who understood military discipline, he was welcomed by staff and pupils alike whenever an extra pair of hands was needed.

To save the school's hard-pressed budget, he also used the mobility vehicle to which Owen was entitled as another means of transport for him and his friends on official trips and outings.

At home, he became what Colleen called a 'backseat pan driver' – cooking and baking for the family – plus he took up cycling and set up his own company, Haatchi Designs, making fun and brightly coloured fabric dog collars and leads. It was a huge mental adjustment, but according to Colleen he became 'the perfect mum and dad rolled into one. Now, at last, he can be the best he can be for Owen, Haatchi and me.'

Being at home full-time also gave Will more opportunity to research Owen's condition on the internet. Because Schwartz-Jampel syndrome is so rare and affects everyone who has it differently, there are few support groups, which can lead to an incredible sense of isolation for the families of those involved. Some become clinically depressed.

Through research that both he and Kim had done when Owen was first diagnosed, however, they had made contact with a few people around the world who had some direct experience of the syndrome. Via emails and the occasional telephone or Skype call, they had been able to share their experiences and raise awareness of the rare condition.

Now, thanks to growing global awareness about Haatchi and Little B, Will and Colleen were contacted by the family of a teenager in France who was quite severely disabled and confined to a wheelchair. They were also approached by the parents of a little boy who was initially misdiagnosed and had undergone seventeen operations on his legs and feet, including bone extensions, before doctors realized that Schwartz-Jampel syndrome was the cause of his problems. Until his family saw Owen and Haatchi on the TV news after their win at Crufts, they thought their son was the only one in the world with the syndrome.

Although the muscle contractions often worsen with age, Owen's family were encouraged by the experiences of a man in the US with Schwartz-Jampel syndrome who led a normal life and drove a car. He was married and the only telltale sign of the syndrome was his facial expression.

Through an SJS support group, the family also made contact with Liz Guidry, originally from Iowa but then living in Suffolk with her husband Bobby, a navigator in the US Air Force. Liz had been diagnosed with SJS at the age of two after she had trouble swallowing and showed signs of stiffness in her leg muscles that affected her mobility. A German doctor who happened to be on duty in her home town knew of the syndrome but had never seen a case before. He prescribed over-the-counter pain relief and, from an early age, Liz learned to 'push on through the pain'. Stretching helped and she never needed the muscle-relaxants on which so many SJS patients rely.

The only outward indication that Liz had the syndrome was that her facial muscles were pulled tight, making her eyes squint. She also had droopy eyelids for which she might eventually require surgery. She said that having a passport photo taken was a nightmare, because each one looked as if her eyes were shut and so they got rejected.

Liz had poor vision and dental problems, tired easily and was unable to kneel or sit for long because of arthritic knees. She fell whenever her knees gave way, limped when she was tired, couldn't lift anything heavy or do any sporting activities. At night she had difficulty breathing if she lay on her back. She was, however, believed to be the first SJS patient in the world to have given birth to a baby – even though the experience drained her. She and her husband had undergone extensive genetic tests to make sure that there was no chance of their child having SJS. Their daughter, Autumn, was born early by Caesarean section after Liz's constricted stomach muscles began to prevent the baby from growing normally in the womb. She is now a healthy eight-year-old.

'Although I wouldn't wish my disability on anyone,' Liz said, 'I'm happy and I get by. I also know I am very lucky and I often feel guilty even to be a member of the SJS support group. I'm proof that there is hope for a normal life with this syndrome.'

Owen's family also became aware of Ben Elwy, from

Boston, Massachusetts, a boy whose symptoms were probably most similar to Little B's. Ben's mother, Rani, is a professor who teaches health policy in a school of public health. She also writes a blog and articles for medical journals, which is how Owen's mother, Kim, first made contact with her.

Born in 2001 with two large bruises on his head, Ben was a fussy, floppy baby who cried a lot and couldn't roll over. At nine months, his legs were bowed and he couldn't carry his own weight. At ten months, a physical therapist suggested he might have a rare condition, and a month later he was diagnosed with eye and hearing problems, some of which were associated with genetic disorders. By the age of twenty-two months, Schwartz-Jampel syndrome was diagnosed.

Rani told Ben's friends and those of her two daughters (neither of whom was born with SJS) that he was like the Tin Man in *The Wizard of Oz*. 'It's as if he has really strong rubber bands trying to stop his every move,' she explained. 'His muscles are so tight that they are holding back his bones from growing.' She asked the children to try to tense their legs and arms in order to feel about one thousandth of what her son lived with every moment of every day, and then to try to move around or do anything when their bodies were that tight.

By the age of twelve, Ben had undergone twenty-three operations, many to correct his eye problems, but others to extend, repair or prevent damage to his spine, hips and legs. He was fitted with titanium rods to his vertebrae and metal plates to his knees and hips. He sees orthopaedic specialists for his knees, wrists and elbows, and will almost certainly need double hip-replacement surgery. Eight years ago he had to have a tracheotomy to prevent the obstructive sleep apnoea that might otherwise have suffocated him at night, and he has been using a walker since he was two and a wheelchair since he was four. His mother said, 'There is no help for Schwartz-Jampel families. No literature. You are on your own. Every surgery is a road newly travelled for the doctors and for us, and it is impossible to know what to expect. One geneticist we saw had only ever seen two cases in his whole life. No one has any answers, so we just have to share what information we can.'

In spite of his physical and medical limitations and the need for a dedicated nurse to manage his trach tube, Ben leads a relatively normal life, goes to an ordinary school and learns the same things as all his classmates. In the summer of 2013 he attended his first technology summer camp, where he helped devise a new computer game. He likes to ride horses and ski (tethered to an instructor). He plays the piano and drums in his school band and is a member of a chess club that meets at his house. In case he loses all vision, he is also learning Braille.

Rani told Owen's family that Ben knows he is different, but it doesn't occur to him not to try something new. At Tech Camp his teacher described him as a 'lightning rod of happiness' who brightened everyone's week. 'Those words and how they make me feel,' said Rani, 'will be fuelling my internal drive for many moons to come.'

She added that she and her family were delighted to learn about the relationship between Owen and Haatchi. She would have loved to get Ben a pet but she is allergic to dogs. 'Owen is doing so well and seems to be a remarkable little boy,' she said. 'I am so happy that he has such a special companion.'

With every day that had passed since Haatchi came into their lives, Will and Colleen had been grateful for his steadying, calm presence. Because of their work patterns, he had rarely been left alone for long, but he definitely loved having his dad home full-time.

As Will adjusted to his new life, he was helped and inspired by how well the eighteen-month-old dog was adapting too. Haatchi had settled into the Howkins-Drummond family so effortlessly and had just been voted one of the winners of the Endal Awards organized by *Dogs Today* magazine and given to dogs or humans who have done something remarkable or inspirational. The award was to be presented at the London Pet Show at Earls Court in May. Announcing their win in the magazine, Beverley Cuddy, editor of *Dogs Today*, said: 'There's something about seeing Owen and Haatchi together that makes us cry. They're mainly happy tears ... We've never had so many nominations for anyone to be awarded an Endal medal. They've already won every award and accolade you can think of and they've never put themselves forward for any of them ... this is one of those true-life stories that would make a great book or an uplifting, award-winning film.'

Haatchi and Little B were getting used to their fame and were becoming veterans of TV shows and other appearances, but when they were invited on to ITV's British Animal Honours awards ceremony, presented by renowned animal lover Paul O'Grady, they knew they'd made the big time. Designed to honour the UK's most extraordinary animals and the people who dedicate their lives to them, the awards had twelve categories and Haatchi had won the Braveheart Honour. Judges included Virginia McKenna from the Born Free Foundation and Peter Egan from All Dogs Matter – which had first helped to rescue Haatchi. The family was invited to the ITV studios in Elstree in Hertfordshire to meet Paul O'Grady, along with Owen's old friend, Queen guitarist Brian May, who was presenting another award.

The show was pre-recorded and Haatchi was helped around the studio by Will and Colleen using his special lifting harness. On 17 April Paul O'Grady appeared on *The One Show* to promote the awards and introduced a segment featuring Haatchi and Little B, which quickly brought tears to the eyes of presenter Alex Jones.

The awards ceremony aired the following night and was watched by millions. Paul O'Grady introduced the winners of the Braveheart Award with the words: 'Sometimes when you see two friends together, it is hard to imagine them ever being apart, but in the case of Owen and Haatchi they very nearly didn't meet at all.'

The audience was shown a short film depicting Haatchi's terrible night on the railway tracks as they were told, 'There was a good chance that Haatchi would never survive his injuries.' Then Paul O'Grady continued: 'Less than fifty miles away, Owen was struggling to come to terms with difficulties of his own,' before Will and Colleen were shown talking about Owen being in constant pain. Colleen said to camera that Little B was the bravest person she had ever met and that he deserved the right to a great life, like anyone else. 'And it is a miracle that Haatchi is alive,' she added, her voice full of emotion. 'To have overcome what he has overcome is an inspiration to us all. . . I am truly indebted to Haatchi and will never be able to pay him back for what he has done.'

Rupert Grint, the actor who played Ron Weasley in the *Harry Potter* films, presented Haatchi with his Braveheart medal as he and Little B received a standing ovation from the studio audience. (Owen had never seen a *Harry Potter* film after he had declared that the stories were 'boring', but he'd seen photos of Rupert Grint and knew he was famous.) The family said afterwards that Rupert was 'super-friendly' and Owen was now a fan.

When Paul O'Grady saw the audience reaction to the boy and his dog, he told Owen: 'Look at that! You got them all on their feet! They didn't do that for me!' He then got down on all fours to say hello to Haatchi before commenting that Owen's style (in a suit and tie) put him to shame and told him to 'come in your scruff' next time.

Owen was later greeted by Brian May and his wife, Anita Dobson, who posed for photographs with him along with another of the judges, Dame Kelly Holmes. He also met Bob, the cat from the bestselling book *A Street Cat Named Bob*, and his owner James Bowen.

When the photoshoot was over, Little B took himself off to a corner and quietly wrote out his autograph for Brian May. He then waited patiently outside the press room to give it to him. When a minor TV star emerged instead, he assumed Owen was waiting for him, so he asked, 'Do you want my autograph?'

'No,' Little B replied, shaking his head emphatically. 'I'm waiting to give mine to Brian May.'

As the disgruntled actor wandered off, Brian came out and graciously accepted the autograph. He then rushed back to his room to find some anti-badger-cull stickers for Owen and declared him an honorary member of his campaign.

Once again, Little B and Haatchi treated the whole event as if it were a normal part of everyday life. The only indication that Owen was remotely starstruck came later when Will overheard him asking complete strangers if they knew any rock stars. When they replied that they didn't, Little B told them, 'I do. He's called Brian May and I've met him twice. He's my friend!'

Will and Colleen hoped that Haatchi would be able to attend the London Pet Show to receive his Endal Award from Allen Parton, the disabled former Royal Navy officer whose faithful Labrador Endal had been the inspiration for the awards, but after the Animal Honours presentation they weren't so sure. Haatchi was fit and well, but the injuries caused by his slip on the ice in February were taking much longer to heal than anyone had expected. By April, it was clear that something wasn't right with Haatchi's lonely rear leg. As a post on Facebook that week said, his 'ouch ouch' was getting worse.

On the recommendation of Angela Griffiths, the owner of Greyfriars Veterinary Rehabilitation Referrals and the first person to realize that the problem was more serious than they had first thought, Colleen and Will took Haatchi to specialist veterinary surgeons Anderson Moores near Winchester – but only after he'd had special hugs and a 'bravery booster' from Owen.

Within the walls of the refurbished granary, vet and senior partner Andy Moores – a specialist in canine joint replacements – saw Haatchi and decided to investigate further. The CT scans he ordered of Haatchi's remaining rear leg showed exactly why he wasn't making as full a recovery as everyone hoped. His hip was fine, but his leg was severely deformed and would require major surgery. His kneecap was permanently dislocated out of the groove it is supposed to run in, a condition known as a luxated patella. The bones below and above (the tibia and femur) were both bowed and twisted and would need breaking and straightening. The operation Haatchi required would be lengthy, risky and expensive. The rehabilitation and after-care costs would be almost crippling for Will and Colleen.

The vets knew that the couple was already under financial pressure after Will had given up his job. They also knew that Haatchi didn't have any pet insurance that would cover a pre-existing condition such as his. The combination of the thousands of pounds involved for the surgery alone plus the lengthy confinement and residential rehabilitation treatment that he'd require after the operation meant that it would possibly be kinder and easier to put him to sleep.

Andy Moores told them gravely that he would need to review the scans and consider what could be done for Haatchi. They would have to wait a day or two before they learned of his decision.

Will and Colleen had always suspected that Haatchi might need wheels one day and OrthoPets, who'd made his special harness, had already offered to make a brace and wheels for him if the couple decided that was what he required, but they'd hoped to delay that as long as possible because it comes with its own complications.

At this point they really didn't know what to decide. They had always said they would do what they felt Haatchi would want them to do, and that Owen would be a big part of that decision. They would never keep a dog alive just for the sake of it, and although losing Haatchi would be incredibly hard for them all – and for Little B most of all – they felt that Owen had such a brilliant mind that, provided it was explained to him correctly, he might cope better than they themselves would.

Close to tears, they brought Haatchi home and lay on the floor with him – and Owen too – to kiss and hug the big dog that, in just over a year, had come to mean so much to them all. They knew that his operation would cost a small fortune – money they simply didn't have – and besides, they didn't know if they could put Haatchi through months spent in a cage with the possibility of further surgery down the line.

They had a few days' grace before they'd have to decide what to do for the best.

Later that night, Colleen posted the news of Haatchi's diagnosis and the images from his CT scans to his more than thirteen thousand followers on Facebook. The page was soon flooded with messages of support and concern, which they found a huge comfort. People sent healing thoughts and good wishes – along with a few 'freckle kisses', 'puppy prayers' and 'tummy scratches'. Those with veterinary or personal experience gave advice, some offered to help pay towards the surgery if necessary, while most reminded the family how much they had already endured and wished them courage and strength for their latest test.

Rod Hunt from OrthoPets made contact too and offered to speak to their vet about providing any special harnesses or orthopaedic braces Haatchi might need. 'This dog is one in a million,' he told them. 'We want to do all we can. It would tear us to pieces if he didn't make it.'

The following day, Will took a call from Andy Moores who informed him that he thought surgical repair was possible, and that not only had they decided that the £9,000-plus cost of Haatchi's operation would be capped at £4,000, but the insurance company Petplan UK had agreed to cover the first £4,000 of the bill at the special request of *Dogs Today* magazine as part of his prize for the Endal Awards.

Once again, the incredible spirit of Haatchi had somehow helped them to help him overcome the odds.

It still meant that they'd have to find at least £4,000 to pay for his aftercare, but the news was so heart-warming that the family knew then that they would definitely go ahead with the surgery.

'We will forever be indebted to the kindness, generosity and professionalism of all concerned,' said Will. 'Yet again, Haatchi seemed to bring out the best in people and we only hoped that some of his good karma would go around and back to all those who helped him.'

It proved to be quite an emotional week, because on the Saturday the family received a timely home visit from someone they had never expected to meet – Siobhan Trinnaman, the RSPCA inspector who had first found Haatchi on the railway tracks.

Haatchi had already been reunited with Ross McCarthy from Dogs and Kisses at Crufts. He'd also reconnected with Nicola Collinson, the volunteer who had driven him from Harmsworth Hospital to South Mimms Services – and who burst into tears when she saw him again. 'It just struck me then that although my role was insignificant, I had helped save him and find Owen and Will and Colleen,' she said. 'That made me very happy.' Thanks to Nicola, Owen also became the grateful recipient of post-cards from exotic places from her boyfriend Ben, a travelling salesman.

Siobhan Trinnaman – who had been alerted to Haatchi's new situation by one of the vet nurses at Harmsworth Hospital – contacted the family via the internet and asked if she could come and see him. Along with her mother, who wanted to meet the famous Haatchi, she then drove from her home in North London to Basingstoke to be reunited with the dog she had known as 'Stray: E10' – the one she'd never quite been able to get out of her mind.

Colleen watched the moment Haatchi saw Siobhan again, eager to see his reaction as she came through the door. He took one look at her, head cocked, and hurried over to cuddle her as if she were his long-lost mum. He then refused to leave her side. Siobhan's eyes filled with tears, as did her mother's. In both cases they were tears of joy.

'I was really delighted to see him again,' said Siobhan. 'It was emotional, and I know a lot of people find the story really upsetting, but to me it is a happy story with a happy ending. No matter what happened to Haatchi on those railway tracks that night, my feeling was that he was now with Owen and his family and everything had turned out for the best.'

Colleen agreed. It was fantastic for them to be able to thank Siobhan in person, because if it hadn't been for her making the decision to rescue Haatchi that night then things might have been so very different. They were all a bit emotional anyway, but seeing Siobhan snuggle with Haatchi and meet Little B for the first time was an uplifting end to a very dramatic few days.

Talking to Siobhan, the couple learned for the first time that Haatchi had been hit over the head before being laid or thrown on to the track. The story they'd always been told – that he'd been tied to the rails – couldn't be verified, but several who were involved in his care still suspected it was so because they believed he might otherwise have managed to avoid the trains that hit him. Siobhan said that, whether he was tied or not, from where he was found it was evident that he had been placed there deliberately, 'put there to die'.

She told the family that the staff at Harmsworth Hospital had been following Haatchi's progress with interest and were all 'rooting for him'. One vet nurse had stuck up photos and newspaper clippings on the staff noticeboard. Siobhan didn't believe that they could ever have put him to sleep; she claimed that RSPCA staff sometimes resorted to suggesting that a dog was at risk of going on the PTS list just so that they could find it a home more quickly.

Stan McCaskie, the vet who was on duty the night Haatchi was rescued, was more pragmatic about what could have been a very unhappy ending for the injured dog. 'The worst part of my job is putting an animal to sleep,' he said. 'It's bad enough when I am relieving their misery or the animal is terminally ill. But when it's a cat or dog that is perfectly healthy but simply can't be found a home, or has bitten someone, or would become too much of a burden, then that is very hard.

'Even though I may be seasoned and hardened, I often

falter at the last and then I always need to take some quiet time to try to bump myself back again.'

Stan, who has devoted his life to saving animals and became a TV star in his own right during the award-winning *Animal Hospital* series filmed at Harmsworth, had been extremely relieved not to have to make that decision with Haatchi. He was even more delighted to learn of his salvation. When he saw him on television winning an award at Crufts, he thought, 'Hang on a minute – I recognize that dog!' He and his colleague Fiona Buchan said that knowing that Haatchi was so happily settled with the Howkins-Drummond family and had made such a difference in Owen's life 'made it all worthwhile'.

On 11 May, two days before Haatchi's surgery was scheduled to take place, Will and Owen attended the London Pet Show without him to be presented with his Endal Award in the Animal Action Arena. Everyone wanted to know where Haatchi was or how he was doing, and Owen enjoyed answering all their questions and being recognized. He told his dad that he was upset that there wasn't an Anatolian Shepherd in sight and promised to bring Haatchi back the following year to show everyone what a wonderful breed it is.

At the UKGSR stand Owen got to name some cuddly toys for a competition, and then they visited some miniature horses that were smaller than Haatchi. He wheeled his electric chair around like a pro, deftly avoiding the crowds, and told everyone that he especially liked seeing the tropical fish.

When it came time to accept Haatchi's award – a lovely medal – Owen surprised his father by telling him to stay in his chair, be on his best behaviour, and that he would go up to receive it by himself. 'Like a trained dad, he did what he was told!' Owen said later. He was thrilled to receive an iPad as a surprise award.

Little B was introduced to Sir Bruce Forsyth, who was very friendly towards him and extremely interested in Haatchi. Sir Bruce was there to support his daughter, Debbie Matthews, who had won an award for her Vets Get Scanning campaign to reunite lost dogs with their owners through microchip technology.

They had a lovely day, although Haatchi was most put out at being left behind because of his injury. That day he posted on Facebook: '*No Mummy, I will not forgive you for not letting me go to London with Little B. Speak to the tail stump, the face ain't listening!*'

Never one to be daunted by a challenge, Colleen decided to reinstate the idea of a £1 sponsored walk, this time to help them pay for Haatchi's rehabilitation. On the eve of his surgery she launched the £1 Ouch Ouch Walk, inviting people to sponsor her, Owen and Mr Pixel to walk the five-mile perimeter of Virginia Water Lake in Surrey with family friend Zoe Le Carpentier and her tri-paw dog Pelucchi. Anyone was invited to join them on Sunday, 2 June.

The goal was to raise the £4,000 they'd need for

Haatchi's soaring rehabilitation costs, which would involve at least three weeks' residential care, then further treatments, including hydrotherapy, acupuncture and physiotherapy, for at least six months. Colleen announced that the plan was to keep Haatchi fit and well so that he could 'continue to be a vital part of the life of his best friend, seven-year-old Owen Howkins, and to carry on helping with charity work for many other organizations.' She added that any donation, no matter how small, would be greatly appreciated.

On Facebook, Haatchi posted: '*One more sleep until my operation. If you have a single pound that you would like to donate toward my rehabilitation . . . then please join our event. Thank you woofy muchly!*'

Will and Colleen drove Haatchi to the vet's early in the morning on 13 May to leave him in the capable hands of the staff. Accompanied by Harold Hedgehog, the toy he was rarely without, he was nevertheless alarmed to be back outside a place that clearly troubled him. While Will went inside to chat to the vets, Colleen stayed out in the car park with her big boy, who – uncharacteristically – didn't even bark at any other dogs that day.

The front door opened and a vet nurse came out with a dog whose belly was shaved and whose rear leg was bandaged. Haatchi's nose shot up and he was overcome with concern, as if suffering a flashback to Harmsworth and his first night in the care of the RSPCA. The smell of anaesthetic started to get to him and he began to whimper. Colleen wondered if he might even try to make a run for it.

Then the door opened again and Andy Moores, Haatchi's surgeon, emerged with Will and ruffled the dog's ears playfully. They followed him inside and then all the way to the surgical kennels, passing uniformed staff who greeted their superstar with warm smiles and kind hands. When they entered the kennel quarters Andy directed them towards a large cage filled with fluffy white blankets. Haatchi was surrounded by other dogs in smaller kennels, but he didn't bark at any of them. He seemed highly suspicious.

Halfway towards his cage, suddenly Haatchi froze in his tracks and appeared to be hit by a wave of fear. He was whining, as if painful memories had come flooding back to haunt him, and it was only when Colleen buried her face in his neck and kissed both his ears that he calmed a little.

They finally managed to get him into his kennel and then they placed Harold Hedgehog next to his nose. He sniffed the fluffy toy, which had spent the previous night in bed snuggled by Owen, and seemed comforted by the familiar smell – so much so that they were able to close the kennel door and leave him in the care of Andy and his team.

Colleen and Will waited until they were outside the building before finally letting go of their emotions at having to leave him there.

The next few hours were extremely tense in the Howkins-Drummond household. Owen was unusually quiet without his big buddy and hardly said a word as they waited for news – that was, until Andy rang to say that the more than five hours of surgery had gone well and there were no side-effects from the anaesthetic. Little B punched the air with his tiny fist and cried, 'Yay!'

The operation involved breaking Haatchi's bones and realigning them with the help of four plates and thirty-four screws to hold everything in place. He had had a 3D model of Haatchi's leg made from the CT scan and had used it to rehearse the surgery prior to the real thing; given the stakes, he didn't want to find out halfway through that he and his team weren't going to be able to achieve a straight leg. Technically it was challenging, but what made it so important was that this was Haatchi's only back leg. If the operation failed, or if there were severe complications, then he wouldn't be able to manage. Also, the vets were working in the knowledge that thousands of Haatchi's fans were waiting and watching to make sure they got him back in one piece to the family. As Andy said, 'No pressure, then!'

Andy promised that his team would monitor Haatchi closely overnight and ring the family back in the morning. The big dog wasn't out of the woods yet, but he was a few steps closer to the long road home.

The following day the nurses reported that he'd managed to eat some food after a good night's sleep and was able both to walk (assisted with a sling) and to move his rear leg, which pleased his surgeon enormously.

His relieved mum and dad posted a photo of Haatchi on his feet showing off his freshly shaved leg and 'baldy bot-bot' on Facebook, along with X-ray images of his new bionic leg peppered with metal pins. They joked: '*I seem to have woken up to a slight case of pins and needs BOL!!! [Bark Out Loud]*'. They also claimed that he was now '*3G and wi-fi enabled*'.

Once he was discharged to the care of Greyfriars, Colleen and Will took turns to visit Haatchi in his kennel at the rehabilitation centre and give him enough cuddles to last him until their next visit. He wasn't amused at having to wear a fabric collar to stop him licking his wounds, but he was sleepy from his pain medication and soon dozed off, snoring, in their laps.

Back home, their bungalow seemed empty without Haatchi. Colleen posted on her Facebook page: '*Coming home from work was so different today. Normally greeted by a big fat fluffy face staring out of the window followed by trying to get through the lounge door and being blocked by a Haatchi huggle with a tail stump wiggling a million miles an hour. Then as soon as I sit down a big fluffy butt plonking itself next to me with two front paws still on the floor and a face with big doe eyes non-verbally asking me how was my day. Ruddy dogs and their innate ability to turn us into helpless mush! Grrr.*'

Owen asked after Haatchi every day and the house just wasn't the same without his enormous, calming presence. Haatchi's little friend didn't rush in from school like he used to, and was markedly subdued, not even wanting to play his favourite Nerf gun game with his dad, and going to bed early. It reminded his family of the quiet days before the Anatolian Shepherd had come into their lives.

Five days after his operation, Haatchi finally had the one visitor he was most looking forward to seeing. Under strict supervision so that he didn't move too suddenly or do anything to damage his leg, Haatchi rolled around the lawn with his best friend Owen. Staff were amazed how much the subdued dog in their care lit up in Little B's presence as he placed a front leg firmly over Owen's body and pulled him towards him in a smiling, panting, huggle.

Cuddles from staff were all right.

Cuddles from Colleen and Will were always welcome.

But nobody cuddled Haatchi like Owen, and the two of them pressed their heads together and stared into each other's eyes with nothing but love.

Over the next few weeks, Haatchi continued to make progress and Colleen kept all his followers informed through postings on his social network sites about Mummy Monday, Freckle Friday and Throwback Thursday. The whole family continued to climb into his cage with him or help him out on to the back lawn for playtime. He publicly pleaded for more treats and was photographed looking aloof with Will and the caption 'No treat? No speak . . .' Another shot showed him lying on the grass with Angela Griffiths, supposedly negotiating a weekend pass home.

By 20 May, less than three weeks after they'd started the campaign, the family had reached their target of raising £4,000 for his rehabilitation. In agreement with all concerned, they kept the page open for extra donations that would be set aside to help subsidize future emergency rehabilitation treatments involving rescue dogs. In all, they raised just over £4,800.

Haatchi was allowed home for the first time on May Bank Holiday weekend, installed in a huge wooden kennel or 'bedroom', purpose-built by Will (with a lot of help from Owen), which dominated the family dining room. Once it was ready, Little B could hardly wait to kick off his shoes and get inside with his furry friend, and was soon snuggled down on Haatchi's bed, demanding a bedtime story. His dad posted a cheeky photo of the two of them behind bars with the caption: '*We are celebrities, get us out of here!*'

The day Haatchi's page reached fourteen thousand likes on Facebook was the day Colleen, Owen and Mr Pixel were due to complete the Ouch Ouch Walk around Virginia Water. After a long, wet month the sun shone and more than thirty friends (and their dogs) turned up to support them. Will made special plaited wristbands for everyone who took part and Little B signed autographs and gave out hugs to anyone who asked.

Among those who turned up – all the way from Rhode Island in America – was Jodi Kennedy, a former journalist and television news anchor who now had a high-profile job in global communications. She had become one of Haatchi's friends on Facebook and was so taken with his story and that of Little B that she began to follow their progress devotedly. She and her husband, Peter, had booked a holiday in France but diverted to the UK just to meet Haatchi and Owen in person and to take part in the sponsored walk. 'I'm sure they feared I was some lunatic stalker from the States,' said Jodi. 'I have never done anything like this in my life before or since.' She explained how it was something about Haatchi's expressive face that had first drawn her to him, plus his graciousness in dealing with the cruelty he had suffered and his subsequent disability. 'Then there was this entire overlay of how he'd saved Owen too, and how generous and admirable Will and Colleen were. They are teaching Owen – and all of us – such incredible lessons about being grateful for what we have, about humility and about giving back.'

Colleen was delighted to meet Jodi and Peter and was more than happy to agree that they could be Owen and Haatchi's 'international godparents'. The couple completed the walk with the rest of the family's many supporters, and everyone went home happy in the knowledge that Haatchi's rehabilitation and care were covered for the next few weeks at least.

In the following week there was a big day for Haatchi. He was taken to the hydrotherapy pool for the first time since his surgery, a move that had to be handled with great care. His entire family was present and Owen took photographs of him exercising in the full-size swimming pool under the constant supervision of two trained physiotherapists in wetsuits. Even the student vets came out of their anatomy class to watch him splashing about in the warm water.

Later in the week, Haatchi tried out the water treadmill for the first time – a device that allowed him to be minimally load-bearing as he used his hind leg. The hydrostatic pressure of the water also reduced any swelling and he loved playing with the floating toys as a physiotherapist massaged his leg and hip under water.

His reward? Another weekend home with his family. Veterinary staff said that his recovery rate had soared since he'd been reunited with Owen and they were keen for his improvement to continue.

As Haatchi and Little B made the front page of the June edition of *Dogs Today* magazine (as well as an inside spread), all seemed to be going well for Will, Colleen and family. They had faced up to the possibility of losing their beloved dog and had overcome it. Owen and Haatchi had been hired as 'roving reporters' for *Dogs Today* and had already written the first blog about their progress under the heading 'Small Miracles and Big Dreams'. In between several other fundraising events for rescue charities, the disabled and individuals, the couple were two months away from their wedding and looking forward to the big day they'd been saving for so hard.

Their friends at the animal food company Natural Instinct, who had offered them free raw food for the whole of Haatchi's life, had left to set up a new company called Nutriment Raw, which the family loyally followed.

Haatchi was making good progress and the fur was growing back on his 'baldy bot-bot'. Owen was doing well at school – especially in maths – and feeling a little better physically because the summer heat eased his joint pain. His mother, Kim, had been deployed to Afghanistan for her fourth tour, but he had always been accustomed to her or Will going away for long periods – happy in the knowledge that they always came back – and he proudly told anyone who asked that she was 'fighting the Taliban'. They chatted on Skype a couple of times a week and he kept her fully informed of all the news about his best buddy.

The family's many friends on Facebook, Twitter and elsewhere, along with pet companies and well-wishers, continued to send them surprise gifts, including Lego and a memory-foam bed (for Haatchi), plus stickers and magnets, books and sweets (for Owen) – all of which were gratefully received.

Then on 25 June there was a major setback.

Haatchi's latest X-rays showed that his tibia and femur were healing but his kneecap was still slipping out of place. Unless Will, Colleen and his therapy teams could build up his muscles with physiotherapy and hydrotherapy to keep the patella stable, he faced further major surgery to realign it, as well as lengthy rehabilitation, all of which was likely to be extremely costly.

As Colleen took on some extra shifts to help meet their growing financial demands, they could only hope and pray that the dog that had changed their lives for the better could have his own happy ending too.

7

'One word frees us of all the weight and pain in life and that word is love.'

Socrates

*H*AATCHI'S DEVOTED TEAM of veterinary staff treated their latest mission to improve his muscle strength as if it were a military operation. Under the leadership of Angela Griffiths, they set to, supervising his almost daily therapy sessions.

To save on costs and to encourage Haatchi to stay in the water for even longer, Will donned goggles and a wetsuit to climb into the pool for the hydrotherapy sessions too. Swimming so often meant that Haatchi was getting stronger and faster every day. Within weeks he was able to swim unaided and without tipping over in the water for the first time since his operation – something he'd mastered quite early on after the loss of his leg. Staff and well-wishers alike were keeping fingers and paws crossed that – with continued therapy – he might be able to avoid further surgery.

Haatchi was growing bored of being in his cage when he wasn't having therapy, though. He rarely whined or barked – unless he needed a comfort break – but he was clearly frustrated at being confined for such long periods, and needed to be distracted. Will and Colleen devised all sorts of games with him that didn't involve much movement – using balls and towels, toys and chews that they could toss around his cage or play tug-of-war with. They moved him from his cage to the lawn, where physiotherapist Kate Vardy massaged and manipulated him, and Little B did his bit too, spending hours with his dog in and out of his cage – even reading and doing his homework next to his furry friend or using him as a backrest.

As Haatchi nuzzled and tickled him (sparking Owen's infectious Woody Woodpecker laugh), Colleen took dozens of photographs of them, along with some of Haatchi wearing his beloved Harold Hedgehog on his head, or rolling on his back, legs akimbo, groaning. In one shot, where he was giving Owen a tongue bath, the caption she posted said: '*Watch and learn, Little B, see, this is a Monday face, you are displaying a Friday face . . . SIGHS . . . the boy has so much to learn!*'

To keep up morale back home, Angela Griffiths gave Owen a toy dog named Hatch that was a model of the dog from Henry VIII's warship, the *Mary Rose*. Hatch had been the official ratter and unofficial mascot on board the vessel, a mongrel whose DNA later proved that he was half Terrier, half Whippet and was under two years old when the ship sank in 1545. His bones were found inside the carpenter's cabin and reassembled as part of the *Mary Rose* exhibition in Portsmouth. Hatch joined the Duchess of York's Corgi, along with the numerous other soft toys almost permanently arranged on Little B's bed.

No one had any idea when Haatchi's real birthdate was, but his first vet had told Will and Colleen that from his teeth he must have been approximately seven months old when they got him, which meant he was born some time in July 2011. As seventeen is Colleen's lucky number, they decided to set the date as 17 July, so that his second birthday would fall exactly one month before their wedding day, which was set for 17 August.

When they posted about his birthday on the internet, they received scores more good wishes for a happy day and a speedy recovery. In typical style, though, the family asked that instead of sending gifts, well-wishers donate money to a friend in need. Colleen wrote on behalf of Haatchi: '*After much thought we have decided to celebrate [my birthday] by doing what we love to do best – helping people.*' She went on to explain that Matt Elworthy, the brother of a friend of hers, had been diagnosed with brain cancer and needed to raise money for life-extending treatment. '*Instead of buying me gifts my family are going to donate £1 each to Matt's Just Giving page and would like to invite you to join us. The treatment means he will have the chance to see his 6-month-old daughter celebrate her first few birthdays, which we think is worth more than all the money in the world . . . Thank you so much. Your generosity will be the bestest birthday gift I could ever hope to have.*'

Soon afterwards, at the new headquarters of Nutriment Raw in Camberley, the family held a joint open day and birthday party for Haatchi. Fans and friends could not only meet him and Little B but also see where and how the company that provided his raw food made their products. There was a huge turnout, including a reunion with James Hearle from Dogs and Kisses, Sara Abbott (who'd painted Haatchi's portrait), and the making of a new friend named Donna who presented them with a beautifully iced cake depicting Haatchi and Little B reading together. That was yet another instance of the spontaneous generosity from strangers that the pair seemed to trigger.

Another had been the kindness of Fiona Simpson, originally from Scotland but now living in the wilds of Norway. She had seen Haatchi and Owen on Facebook and was charmed by them winning the Crufts Friends for Life Award. Fiona spent her spare time making papier-mâché and woollen 'doggiebears' as gifts for friends or to auction for animal charities, so she crafted a special three-legged, freckle-nosed Haatchibear and sent it to the Howkins-Drummond family. They were thrilled and quickly posted a photograph of it on their social networking sites. Fiona was then inundated with enquiries from people wanting their dogs crafted in wool and/or a Haatchibear of their own. She felt it was wrong to make a commodity out of him, and she knew that the family did a lot of work for charity, so she suggested she make one and auction it for a charity of their choice.

Haatchi and Owen picked the Muffin's Dream Foundation for handicapped children and their families, and the first auction on eBay raised £105. 'I can't afford to give money to charity,' said Fiona, 'but this is my way of doing something.' Since that auction, she has been bombarded with further requests and orders for her £30 doggiebears as the Haatchi karma continues to work its special magic. She plans to make and auction more Haatchibears in the future for whichever charity Owen and Haatchi select.

Another group who fell for Haatchi and Owen were student filmmakers and dog lovers Jonna McIver, Carl Frazer-Lunn and Jodi Rose Tierney at the University of Hertfordshire. The trio initially spotted Haatchi on the internet and then in early 2013 approached the family via Facebook to ask if they would consider featuring in a short film as part of the final-year media assignment in their degree in Film and TV Production. Will and Colleen immediately agreed, so director and producer Jonna, accompanied by Carl on camera and editing, and Jodi as assistant director and sound, went to meet them.

'We'd seen their photographs and thought they both looked incredible,' explained Jonna. 'We also thought that their story was too good not to film – both Owen's condition and all that Haatchi had to overcome. Nothing prepared us for how special they were together, though.'

Owen was at school when they arrived, so they met Haatchi first and were amazed by how big he was and also how calm. There was, Jonna said, 'something exceptional' about him that was hard to define. 'Then Owen came home and we could immediately see the bond between them. And he was incredible. At seven years old he was offering us cups of tea and asking if we needed anything. All the while he sat right up close to this enormous dog who watched his every move.'

The documentary team instinctively knew that they had struck filmic gold. For the next two months, they followed the family around doggedly (as Haatchi would say). They filmed Little B playing with Haatchi and their toys, relaxing at home and out in the local park. Their camera was running as the muscle-bound boy struggled to move from his walker to his wheelchair. Planning to over-dub childlike illustrations of a sad-looking Haatchi next to a railway line, they asked Owen to face the camera and provide the commentary.

'Here's a story . . . Haatchi got hit by a train,' Little B said. 'The RSPCA found him and then Ross and James adopted him. Then he was feeling bad and then he came to us!' With a sigh he added: 'He does look after me and he's special . . . I feel really happy. Everything changed in my life then . . . I was scared of strangers but he changed my life to not be scared of things now.'

The crew hadn't yet decided how to finish their film when the family heard that they were to be in the final of the Friends for Life Awards at Crufts. The Kennel Club gave the students full access so that they could film their happy ending as Owen accepted his prize.

'It was so humbling to see a child who is in pain twenty-four/seven being so bubbly and happy,' said Jonna. 'You would never know how much everything hurts him. We ended up forging a really great relationship with him and the rest of the family and were just so pleased to have seen the real Owen, the one who lights up a room when he knows you and isn't being shy.'

Jonna, who hopes to become a professional documentary director, said his biggest task was to decide which shots to cut as there was so much great material, including an emotional Howkins-Drummond family being presented with Haatchi's portrait by Sara Abbott. They were pleased to be able to use some of the funniest outtakes during the credits, in which Little B fooled around making his hand disappear up his sleeve, explained how happy he was, and put a blob of melted chocolate on his nose while baking with his dad.

On 4 June (while Haatchi was still in residential rehabilitation) Will, Colleen and Owen travelled to Hatfield to support their new friends as their nine-minute documentary – entitled *A Boy and His Dog* – was entered for the ITV Award for a Documentary at the university's 2013 Visions Festival. After watching all the other contenders for entertainment, fiction and documentary films, and being amazed by the quality and varied subject matter, everyone was thrilled when *A Boy and His Dog* won the documentary first prize, bringing tears to the eyes of many of the several hundred people in the audience – including Will and Colleen.

For one night at least, everyone had their happy ending.

And there was more good news to come when the film was also nominated for the BAFTA Short Film Award, to be decided in 2014.

It was around this time that Owen started to complain that his hips were hurting. His father knew that, because of the strong anti-convulsive and muscle-relaxants he was taking daily, Little B must really have been in pain to have felt something new. They took him back to Southampton General Hospital for some tests, after which the doctors decided to X-ray his hips for the first time in five years. The images that were subsequently produced were even more shocking than the ones they had recently been shown of Haatchi's badly bowed rear leg.

Seeing the deterioration in his son's bones marked one of the worst days of Will's life.

Owen's orthopaedic specialists had warned that he might need both hips replaced multiple times during his life, but suggested that this wouldn't happen until he'd stopped growing – probably in his late teens. Before they could assess him fully this time, though, they wanted to take some more detailed CT scans of his lower body.

To keep Little B fully informed and as a treat he was allowed into the hospital's radiography room to view those scans and watch the 3D images of his hip joints panning up on the screen.

As Will and Colleen looked on in silence they saw for

the first time that both Owen's hips were dislocated due to the continual pressure of the muscles contracting around them, and one of the ball joints had been worn down to half its size. Seeing those stark black-and-white images of his seven-year-old son's skeletal condition brought it home to Will how far they had yet to go. 'The deterioration was incredible,' he said. 'Anyone else would have been crying out in pain, but Owen has a much higher threshold than normal.'

Even if his hips had been checked sooner and he'd been put through painful reconstruction surgery, his consultant Michael Uglow believed that it wouldn't have made a difference due to the strong muscle pull.

'Because of the severe nature of his condition,' he said, 'it's a real possibility that if I'd recommended reconstruction some years ago Owen's hips might still have subsequently dislocated anyway. I'm quite relieved that we're not in a situation where we had failed surgically having put him through very major surgery.' He added that unless there are significant changes in implants, such as magnetic joints to prevent them dislocating, he couldn't see that replacements would ever be realistic in Owen's case.

The blood supply to Little B's hips was another major cause of concern. The orthopaedic specialists were worried that there might be an insufficient or impaired blood flow to the joints and they needed to carry out further tests. The fear was that more cells of the bone tissue might die without proper circulation – a condition known as necrosis, which can lead to the total collapse of the joint.

Owen's original consultant, Dr Thomas, admitted later that Owen might well become less mobile and require what he called 'troublesome surgical intervention'. The doctor added that he'd always hoped that wouldn't be the case, especially in 'such a cheerful little chap' who always had something funny to say. However, he had always told the family that it was impossible to say what lay ahead for Owen, given his deterioration in the last few years. The doctor's hope was that Little B's physical development and growth might alter or favourably affect that course in the future.

'It's always such a pleasure to see Owen,' he said, 'and what I especially like about him is that he is so un-complaining for someone who is not able to do a lot of the things he should be doing at his age. His family have had a tough old time and they push for the best for him, but never in an unreasonable way.'

All the doctors could offer Owen for the time being were deep-tissue steroid injections every six months, which would have to be done under general anaesthetic. The date for the first one was booked for August – one week after Will and Colleen's wedding.

Little B had already been through so much in his short life, but he had coped with each new setback admirably thanks to the love and support of his family – and Haatchi. When his muscle-relaxants first affected his sight and his balance, he'd struggled on regardless. Moving from a walker to a wheelchair had been a major step, but with everyone's help Owen had turned even that into a positive. Then he'd had to adapt to using oxygen every night, as well as taking even more medicines for the constant stomach problems that were a side-effect of both his drugs and the syndrome.

Now, he faced the biggest challenge of all – his first major surgery and the reduction or even loss of what little mobility he had. Will and Colleen knew what the doctors were trying to tell them but they could hardly take it in. When they eventually left the hospital with him, Will was too upset to drive home.

The next day he contacted the few people he knew around the world with direct experience of Schwartz-Jampel syndrome to ask if any of them had problems with their hips. Almost all of them told him they had. Many had gone through replacement operations, and the dislocation of joints seemed common, along with loss of mobility.

With characteristic fortitude, Little B took in what little information he'd been given and worked it all out in his young head. Back home, he crawled into the kennel where his beloved Haatchi was recovering from the major operation to his leg. Owen had seen how stoically his dog had endured the pain and frustration of the previous few weeks and was quietly inspired by him.

In one of their many secret conversations as they huggled together gently, Owen told his best buddy that he, too, might have to have surgery. If so, what finer example could there be for the brave little boy to learn from? By the time he was sleepily ready for his bed, Little B seemed to have decided that he and Haatchi would somehow work through their problems together – just as they always had.

Once again, Will and Colleen couldn't help thinking that fate had brought the little boy and the big dog together. They sincerely hoped that the remarkable connection they shared would sustain them through the difficult times ahead.

Fortunately, the family had something wonderful to look forward to – a summer wedding. After all they'd been through since Will first posted a smiley face on Colleen's profile page four years earlier, this was the day they'd all been waiting for.

From the day he asked her to be his bride in Scotland in the summer of 2010, the couple had been determined to include Owen in every aspect of their wedding plans. Will had even sought his son's advice about the engagement ring. With such a wise head on his young shoulders, the couple knew instinctively that Little B would be an invaluable asset to the whole process. They also wanted it to be as much his day as theirs.

Their marriage wouldn't change much about their everyday lives, except that Colleen would officially become Owen's stepmother. 'It must be confusing for a child from a broken home whose mother is away working a lot, but thankfully we hit it off right from the start,' she said. 'Only once did he ask me if he could call me "Mum" and I gently told him that he already had one. Sometimes when he's being cheeky he might call me "Mummy", but I'll give him a look that says I don't approve. It is important that he knows that Kim is his mother. It is not something for her to give up or for me to take. She is the reason he is here and I will always be eternally grateful to her for that.'

The couple began to search for a wedding venue where they could have the ceremony and the reception all in the same place. They took Owen with them to view possible sites. They needed it to be as flat as possible so that he had easy access and could use his walker and his wheelchair. It had to be within easy driving distance to either Basingstoke or Southampton Hospitals in case he was taken poorly. Ideally, it should also be not too far from their bungalow so that they wouldn't have to deal with the logistics of installing an oxygen machine if they stayed over.

Colleen had seen TV shows where women spent thousands and turned into 'bridezillas', and she didn't want anything like that. She and Will just hoped for an old-fashioned romantic day with flowers and candles and a handful of carefully chosen guests. They thought they'd found the perfect place that could be candlelit, but when they made the decision for Will to leave the RAF they had to abandon that venue because of the cost. With just one wage coming in, money was tight and although they recognized that there were a lot of people worse off than they were, they did have to think carefully about things and they wanted to be sure they were getting married for the right reasons. In her straightforward New Zealand style, Colleen reminded herself that the wedding was 'just a meal and a drink before we sign a bit of dead wood to tell the world we love each other'.

Cutting back on what was a 'want rather than a need', the couple determined that the most important thing was for Owen to have a lovely day. They decided on a much smaller event to celebrate spending the rest of their lives together. After searching around, they came across Barton's Mill, a friendly pub in a converted watermill on the banks of the River Loddon in Old Basing, fifteen minutes from their home. It had a lake and there was an old-fashioned restaurant attached. It held a civil wedding licence and was mainly on one level, so it seemed perfect, but Will and Colleen were still concerned about the cost. They took Owen and Haatchi to see it for the first time, and the owners were so taken with them all that they offered the venue at a discount, which suddenly made it affordable.

Sitting out on the front lawns having a drink together to celebrate finally having found the perfect location for their wedding, Will, Colleen and Little B couldn't have been happier. Now that they had the place figured out, they simply had to decide on all the details, and Colleen couldn't wait to get started as they chatted excitedly about their plans. There would be around fifty guests at the ceremony and reception and then another fifty at an evening party. The pub gardens were situated a few hundred yards from a red-brick Victorian viaduct that spans the river and would provide the perfect backdrop for photographs.

Haatchi lay alongside them quite happily as they talked, but suddenly he sat up, tensed his muscles and started trembling all over. Colleen and Will noticed it immediately and wondered if he had eaten something that upset him. Then, as she went to stroke him, Colleen heard something that made her own blood run cold.

'Oh, God!' she cried. 'It's a train. A train's coming across the bridge! He can hear it!'

Ever since they'd rescued Haatchi they had been careful never to take him to a train station or near a railway line in case he suffered some sort of flashback. At Barton's Mill they inadvertently found themselves sitting beneath a huge viaduct that carried the main London to Plymouth line via Basingstoke. Up until that moment, they hadn't even appreciated the place was close to a railway.

As a dog trainer, Colleen knew instinctively that the way they handled the next few minutes would be vital to Haatchi's future. Turning away from the cowering animal, she said under her breath to Will and Owen, 'Whatever you do, don't look at him and don't react!'

Deeply concerned for their beloved pet, it took all their willpower not to reassure him as he quivered and quaked at the sound of the approaching locomotive that must have reminded him of that cold night in January when he'd almost died.

Out of the corner of her eye, Colleen saw Haatchi look

anxiously from her to Will to Little B as the train passed directly overhead. His ears were flat and his stump of a tail was firmly tucked down. As they held their collective breath, the train rumbled past and Haatchi finally stopped shaking. Then he tilted his head quizzically as he registered with apparent surprise that not only was he still alive but that none of his family seemed to be in the slightest bit afraid.

Looking up at them as if to say, 'Hey, nothing happened!' he seemed to shrug his doggie shoulders before slumping back down on to the grass to lick his paws, confident that he was safe.

It was a scary moment – for all of them. It was also a very emotional one. In his fear, Haatchi could easily have run from the noise, which would have done untold damage to his leg. Colleen knew that they would never have been able to hold him if he'd really wanted to flee. Instead he had trusted them to keep him from harm, and he had demonstrated yet again that, although one human being had done something terrible to him, he had forgiven all of humanity.

8

'*To have and to hold from this day forward, for better for worse,
for richer for poorer, in sickness and in health, till death us do part.*'

Traditional marriage vows

MONTHS OF CAREFUL planning had gone into what Will
and Colleen hoped would be the best day of their
lives. As soon as they had the date and the venue booked,
they began to think about everything else that needed to
be organized.

Colleen's beloved Aunt Tui was flying in from Australia
to walk her down the aisle. Tui's middle name is Colleen,
so she had been named after her. Her first name is that of
a popular New Zealand bird of the honeyeater family.
Some of Colleen's happiest childhood memories revolved
around her aunt, and she couldn't wait to see her again
and introduce her to the incredible new family she'd
become a part of.

The whole wedding was to be a family affair, because
even their florist, Sue Pritchard, was related. She was the

mother-in-law of Will's sister Esther, and she specialized in just the kind of old-fashioned roses, herbs and wild flowers the couple wanted. The aisle leading to the area where the vows were to be taken would be decorated with miniature lavender trees, and the tables at the reception would be adorned with fresh mint, rosemary and bay leaves. Colleen's bouquet was to be made of dusky pink roses – one called Peace and the other Amnesia – and Will and Owen would wear matching roses in their buttonholes.

Food was very important to them both: they wanted good, rustic fare with nothing too fancy, and Barton's Mill provided a perfect three-course menu, with a full buffet in the evening. Their wedding cake was a three-tiered vision in dusky lilac icing with white lace sugar flowers and butterflies, and the bakers also made special bone-shaped cookies for Haatchi.

Colleen was booked to stay at a local four-star hotel named Audleys Wood with her two bridesmaids, her mother, her aunt and some girlfriends the night before the wedding, which meant that the chauffeur of the 1929 Austin 12 car they'd hired could take Will, Little B and Haatchi to the venue first before doubling back for her.

Jenny Hawkes, a longstanding friend, was one bridesmaid and Jenny's husband Zaren was their usher. Her other bridesmaid was her friend and colleague Lisa Ford.

Colleen had always wanted a wedding dress that was different from other gowns. She didn't care too much for traditional white or ivory and eventually found just what she wanted online – a dusky pink raw silk dress with a lace bodice by Australian designer Mariana Hardwick. Her bridesmaids wore matching chiffon gowns.

When her grandmother Sylvia had passed away, Colleen's mother had told her to choose anything she wanted from her effects. She looked around the room and felt she could almost hear Sylvia directing her to a small box, which contained a silver filigree brooch in the shape of a butterfly. Butterflies have always been very special to Colleen, so she picked that piece of jewellery and it has become her most precious possession. For her 'something old' she attached it to the pink satin fabric of her shoe so that she could feel that her grandmother was walking down the aisle with her. The bridal gown was her 'something new', in which there was a 'blue' label, and she 'borrowed' a ribbon for a wrist decoration. In her hair she would wear diamanté butterfly clips and seed pearls.

Will and Little B had hired matching slate-grey morning suits, complete with coat tails, ivory embroidered waistcoats and pink cravats. Owen was to keep the simple gold bands in a special pocket in his waistcoat.

The couple had a lot of fun choosing the music for their special day. They were determined to include some humour in what would undoubtedly be an emotional ceremony for all concerned, so they made sure that alongside the songs that meant the most to them they also had a couple of more light-hearted choices. After 'Stand By Me' by Ben E. King, Colleen would come down the aisle to the song 'I Will Love You' by an artist known as Fisher.

She'd first come across it when it was posted on Facebook by a canine friend of Haatchi's who goes by the name of Malibu Thomson, Love Ambassador for the Elderly. To lighten proceedings in case they became too soppy, the couple had arranged to come back down the aisle to 'I Fought the Law and the Law Won' by The Clash.

They would be married by a local registrar and, as well as making the traditional wedding vows, they each had personal statements to read to each other that would almost certainly trigger tears – if only in each other. Film-makers Jonna and Carl from Hertfordshire University would capture every moment on video.

Among those invited to their special day along with their family, friends and colleagues would be David and Suzanne Brock and Michael McVeigh. Angela Griffiths from Greyfriars was there along with Joanne Cleeve, Haatchi's first massage therapist, whom he'd met at Crufts. Sue Crilly, from UK German Shepherd Rescue, a friend they'd made since taking on Haatchi, would be looking on and Jodi and Peter Kennedy were flying in specially from the USA to be there as well.

When they'd first decided to get married, Colleen and Will thought that instead of having a wedding gift list – they felt they already had everything they needed – they would ask their friends and family if they might like to contribute to a special holiday for Owen. The couple hoped to take him somewhere that he was still young enough to enjoy but old enough to appreciate, so they came up with the idea of visiting Santa Claus in Lapland just before Christmas. They knew the logistics with his oxygen and accessibility would take some organizing, but they both felt it would be worth it. 'Not to be fatalistic, but we don't know what Owen's long-term prognosis is and we'd like him to have as many wonderful memories as possible,' said Colleen. They decided to erect a special secret postbox at their reception for people to drop their contributions into. The whole thing was to be a huge surprise for Little B, so everyone was sworn to secrecy.

Happy with their decision, and thankful that Haatchi and Little B were both in reasonable health as they continued to plan their wedding, the couple hoped to be able to save up enough money to treat themselves to a special wedding night in a hotel followed by a proper honeymoon – their first foreign holiday together. As Will had asked Colleen to marry him in a tree house, they were thrilled to discover a beautiful tree house resort in Costa Rica, so they put down a deposit and were looking forward to the trip of a lifetime.

Then they started to have second thoughts.

First, they questioned the expense of staying in a hotel when they had a perfectly comfortable bungalow nearby. If they just went home on their wedding night, they wouldn't have to worry about Haatchi or Little B, both of whom could stay in familiar surroundings and not get unduly stressed. 'Owen was already a bit anxious about being the best man, so we wanted to make everything as stress-free as possible, because stress can cause him to become poorly,' explained Will. So they cancelled the hotel.

Then they began to worry about leaving Owen for two weeks while they were in Costa Rica. At the time they were planning their trip, Kim was about to be deployed to Afghanistan and would almost certainly be abroad. Although he loved staying with his grandparents in Devon, and their chalet bungalow had been specially modified with a ramp and an airflow machine, it was still a lot to ask them to manage over a long period when he needed nightly monitoring.

By the time Haatchi slipped over and hurt himself, Colleen was in an agony of indecision. Who would supervise his care while they were away? They'd spent all his Ouch Ouch Walk money on his care to date and had to fund the rest out of their own resources. Two weeks in residential rehabilitation would be cripplingly expensive. When she began to research how much the Lapland trip would cost for Owen, she was even more alarmed. To take a disabled child with such particular needs on a trip like that is clearly very expensive, but Colleen realized that if they were going to ask people to contribute to it then she and Will couldn't possibly go on an extravagant honeymoon. When she told Will she was going to cancel it and ask for the deposit back he did a double-take. He was so looking forward to their big treat, as was she; but he also knew she was right – a honeymoon was just too much of a luxury.

Having decided not to go abroad, they remembered Jan Wolfe, their Facebook friend who ran dog-friendly self-catering cottages on the Ardmaddy Estate in Argyll, less than an hour from where Will had proposed. They made contact and found that a former ferryman's cottage right next to the loch was available for the last week in August. It meant they could take Haatchi and Mr Pixel with them and not have to shell out for kennel fees. They could eat what they liked, cheaply, and would be in the same country as Owen – who'd be with his grandparents in Devon – in case of any emergencies.

To seal the deal, one week before the wedding they heard from Haatchi's vet Andy Moores that he was delighted with the three-legged dog's progress and would probably not need to perform a second operation after all. The latest examinations had shown that in terms of recovery Haatchi was two weeks further on than Andy had expected, thanks to his diet and all the hydrotherapy, and now he could gradually increase his activity and weight-bearing day by day. He would no longer have to be caged all day and could go on gentle walks and swims with them in Scotland.

Fate had intervened again, and their honeymoon now seemed like it was meant to be.

Will chose to spend what he jokingly referred to as his 'last night of freedom' alone with his son. They went to the cinema to see the 3D animated movie *Planes* and then they ate a burger together before going home to bed. Kissing his son goodnight, he reflected on how far they had come and how lucky they were to have Colleen and Haatchi in their lives.

Colleen had dinner with her bridesmaids Lisa and

Jenny plus friends and family. Her girlfriends had already treated her to a surprise hen night in a London spa hotel, plus a Jamie Oliver cookery course. Colleen's one regret was that her grandparents couldn't be there to share in her happiness. They had been her inspiration and the perfect role models, known for their kindness and generosity. One day Colleen had asked her grandmother what the secret recipe was to a happy marriage. Sylvia told her granddaughter that communication was the most important thing of all, especially listening to the things that you might not really want to hear. Shouting never helped, she said, because nobody heard you. She added that kissing each other on the lips every day was vital and one of the most intimate things a couple could do, as it showed complete and utter trust. She warned Colleen, 'The day you stop kissing each other on the lips is the day your marriage is in serious trouble.' Turning to her grandfather for his words of wisdom, Colleen asked what his recipe for a happy marriage was. Without skipping a beat, he ripped the hearing aid from his ear and said, 'This is! Sorted!'

Colleen and Will's long-awaited wedding day, Saturday, 17 August, dawned grey and cloudy, but nothing could dampen their spirits. When they woke up that morning – in separate locations as tradition dictated – there were nothing but smiles as they put all their troubles behind them.

Bridesmaid Lisa – who also worked as a part-time hairdresser – curled Colleen's hair into ringlets while she checked her recent manicure and pedicure for any blemishes. Jenny helped her get ready.

A few miles away, Will helped Owen dress in his little morning suit, then they fixed a newly plaited purple-and-white collar around Haatchi's huge neck. Will could tell that his son was nervous, so he was pleased he had something to distract him.

Once he was in his suit, he presented Little B with his first proper watch as a gift for being best man. It even triggered a high-five, plus Owen's trademark 'Awesome!' Squinting at it through his glasses, he admired its stylish black rubber design and magnified face, and for the rest of the day proudly offered to tell the time to anyone who was interested.

In the weeks before the wedding the couple had taken Haatchi back to the venue several times to make sure that he was fully accustomed to the sound of passing trains. 'Each time he heard a train approaching, he was fine,' Will said. 'He'd look up, cock his head, check out our reaction and settle back down when he saw that there was none. He's a smart dog and he figured it out all by himself. It seems incredible that we'd only had him eighteen months – it seemed like he'd always been in our lives – but in that time he had somehow come to understand that now he was in our care we would do everything within our power to ensure that nothing could ever hurt him again.'

In the picturesque setting of the watermill, with its industrial cogs and wheels a major feature of the room where they would take their vows, friends and family arrived early to give Will and Owen all the support and encouragement they could. American guests Jodi and Peter Kennedy were delighted to meet everyone and Jodi found the day's events deeply moving. 'There is such a powerful connection to joy with this family,' she said. 'They have been dealt cards that are so challenging and yet they are a wonderfully inspirational example of how to cherish life's gifts and remind us all what is truly important.'

Her husband said that their friends back home thought they were crazy to travel all the way to the UK to attend the wedding of a couple they'd only met online a few months previously. But he added: 'Will, Colleen and Owen have taught us so much. They give back to everyone. We have been so humbled by the way they lead their lives. It has certainly changed ours.'

Colleen's mother, Kathryn, was immensely proud of her daughter and future son-in-law. Watching Owen at the wedding, she said she wouldn't have recognized him as the withdrawn little boy she had first met four years previously. 'He is so sociable and funny now. Thanks to Colleen and Will, and especially Haatchi, he's become so much more outgoing. They make a lovely wee family.'

Aunt Tui, who was resplendent in a feather fascinator, added: 'I met Owen when Colleen and Will first met, but he was terribly fearful of new people then. Now he is completely different and I can't take my eyes off him – the transformation is incredible. I'd heard so much about his big three-legged dog, but to meet Haatchi at last was overwhelming – and what he has done for Owen is amazing. They're both so gorgeous and lovable and unusual.'

Despite the rain, the wedding went off beautifully, although Will couldn't hold back his tears when he saw Colleen walking down the aisle towards him on Tui's arm. The transformation, he said later, was 'breathtaking'. When Tui and the bridesmaids began to cry too, boxes of tissues were quickly handed around. Haatchi defused the emotion by barking loudly and crashing his big front paw – first on to the table and then on Colleen. 'He wasn't used to seeing me all dressed up,' she said later. 'And he certainly wasn't used to seeing me crying. I think when he heard my voice he suddenly realized that the lady in the dress was me and he wanted some attention.'

As Owen took photographs on his grandmother Joan's camera the couple who'd been on their own long journey held hands, faced each other, and – after reciting the official vows – spoke the ones they'd written specially to each other.

Half-laughing and half-crying, Will told his bride: 'I, Will, before these nutters assembled, take this bit of crumpet to be my wife, my friend, my lover, my hot water bottle and my companion in life. I will care for and protect you, nurture you and support you, and tell you when you are being a numpty and adore everything about you.

'I promise to love you tirelessly through perfect times and the merely fabulous times, regardless of how often you get distracted by Facebook or the Crime Investigation channel (which I have to confess makes me a bit nervous, especially when you watch *Deadly Women*).

'I vow above all things to remain unchanged in this, even if I should be momentarily distracted by all of your gorgeous-looking female friends. I vow to understand you when I don't, to admit that I am in the wrong when I mistakenly think I am in the right and to bring you flowers at least once a week, as I am bound to have done something I should apologize for.

'In the presence of these nutt . . . er, our beloved family and friends, I offer you my solemn vow to be your god-like partner and lover; in sickness and in health, in good times and in bad, and in joy as well as in sorrow, I give you my heart, my love, my soul. I love you, now and for ever.'

When the laughter eventually died down, Colleen told her groom: 'You make loving easy. For starters, living in sin was totally worth it. I now know you are able to deal with my annoying habits.

'You pick up my half-empty coffee cups that I leave around the house, you let me sleep in on my days off and you always know where my mobile phone and keys are when I go into full panic mode and scream that someone has hidden them.

'With you I have learned to take it slow, although I could have dealt with getting here a little faster. Only time would allow me to see your true colours. You're generous, loving, sensitive, kind, and a brilliant dad to Owen.'

Choking slightly, she continued: 'I, Colleen, take you to be my husband, my friend, my lover, my hot water bottle, my companion in life and my good cop-bad cop vegetable-patrol partner in Owen's Dinner Crime sprees.

'I will love you unconditionally, support you in your goals, honour and respect you, without TOO much grief (except on Fridays). I will always listen to what you have to say, even when we don't see eye to eye – remember love is saying "I feel differently" instead of "You're wrong" – and continue to love Owen as if he was my own, as I officially become your partner in his life.

'I promise to love you through good times and the merely perfect times, regardless of how often you leave cupboard doors open around the house like a scene from the movie *The Sixth Sense*. I will resist the urge to beat you with the rolling pin when you leave used tea bags on the oak kitchen counters, and to comfort you in times of sorrow, including rough rugby, cricket and football seasons (especially when New Zealand is whipping Britain's butt).

'In the presence of our family and friends who insisted on tagging along, I offer you my solemn vow to be your ever-suffering nurse in sickness and in health, despite your self-inflicted-hangover whining and man-flu dying declarations. But most of all, I promise to love you, under any circumstances, happy or sad, easy or difficult, through the sunshine and through the rain for the rest of my days.

'I am the luckiest girl in the world and I couldn't imagine growing old with anyone else so let's grow old together disgracefully.'

Owen, propped up in his walker in the aisle a few feet

away, kept checking the time on his new watch. Will had given him a military-style timetable of when everything would happen and how long each segment would take, and he wanted to be sure everything was running on time. He kept the wedding bands in a little velvet bag in a special pocket deep within his waistcoat and he got them out and looked at them numerous times before and during the ceremony, to check that they were still safe. When his time came to perform, he solemnly handed over the rings one by one on cue, looking proudly up at his dad.

Then Pat Morgan, the registrar, asked if there was anyone who had any reason why Colleen and Will shouldn't be married, and silence prevailed. She waited – a few seconds longer than usual, everyone thought. Will and Owen had secretly rehearsed that Little B would say, 'No! Get on with it!', but Owen clammed up at the crucial moment. The registrar looked at Will and asked, 'Shall we give it a bit longer?' but Owen resolutely shook his head so the ceremony concluded and even Haatchi didn't object.

Owen also balked at saying one of his favourite lines at the end of the service: 'In the words of Tommy Cooper – "Just like that!"' A spontaneous wit, the seven-year-old flatly refused to perform to order.

There was only one awkward moment. When it came to signing the paperwork for the registrar Colleen was asked to enter her father's full name, but she didn't even know it. Aunt Tui helped her out and then the registrar asked if he was still alive.

'Is he?' Colleen enquired flatly. Her aunt laughed and

nodded, and told the registrar that she'd seen her brother a few weeks previously.

Colleen then asked the registrar if there was any way her mother's name only could be listed on the marriage certificate, but she was told that the law insisted that her father's name was given. Determined not to let anything ruin her day, Colleen simply smiled and did as she was asked.

After the ceremony, the happy couple went outside during a short respite in the rain to chat to their guests and sip champagne before their meal. While they were busy mingling, Little B was taken to one side by Carl and Jonna and asked if he'd like to say a few words to camera for the wedding video. Taking a deep breath, he smiled broadly, looked straight into the lens like a professional, and said: 'Dear Colleen and Daddy, I'm sending you this message to say congratulations and well done. I love you so much and I can't even believe you got married!'

His endearing legacy message was guaranteed to reduce the viewer to tears.

All of Will's family was there to congratulate him, including his three siblings and their seven children. Several made comedy speeches. His sister Esther was heavily pregnant and about to give birth to a boy, Seth. Two months previously, his other sister Bethany had been safely delivered of a baby girl, Ettie, and his brother Ed's wife had a new baby daughter, Ada. With three new grandchildren in one year, Will's mother, Joan, said that although the family knew that Owen's syndrome was a 'fluke' caused by two sets of faulty genes, they were anxious every time a new pregnancy was announced and hugely relieved whenever a healthy baby was born.

The wedding photographer, Nigel Rousell, a former colleague of Colleen's and a family friend, asked the bride and groom if he could take some shots of them under the red-brick Victorian railway viaduct.

'Yes, but I think we'll keep Haatchi out of these ones,' Colleen insisted, as she watched her three-legged rescue dog comfortably settled by the fireplace, blissfully unaware of the proximity of any trains. Knowing that he was safe and happy, she and Will wandered off down a winding gravel path to have the photographs taken to mark their special day.

It was only when they got back to the mill house some time later that Colleen looked down and realized that her grandmother's butterfly brooch was no longer pinned to her shoe. Fighting back the tears, she couldn't believe that she had somehow mislaid her most precious belonging.

The next hour was taken up with a systematic search of the entire venue, grounds, and pathway. Jodi Kennedy – their high-powered friend from the States – kicked off her designer shoes to walk every inch of the wet lawn in the hope that she might feel the brooch with her bare feet. The chauffeur of their vintage car was asked to check the vehicle, and staff and guests were enlisted to conduct an almost fingertip search of every room Colleen had been in.

Desperately worried, but trying not to let it spoil

everything, Colleen kept reassuring herself that the precious brooch would eventually turn up. Then, on the edge of dusk, a keen-sighted girlfriend walked back down the gravel path alone and spotted it glistening in the rain.

Tears of joy quickly replaced those of sadness and Colleen pressed the brooch to her heart. Her mother Kathryn laughed and told her, 'I'm sure that was just your grandmother's little way of saying, "Don't forget me, I'm a big part of this day too!"'

Will ordered a pint of beer to celebrate and insisted he keep the brooch safely in the pocket of his waistcoat. Relieved that the drama was over, he fed Haatchi and arranged for a friend to take him home and put him into his purpose-built 'bedroom' before the evening celebrations began.

Little B kissed his big buddy goodnight and went back to having fun. He'd remained largely oblivious to the missing-brooch saga, not out of a lack of interest but because he was otherwise and very happily engaged. Apart from the excitement of the day, his new watch and being best man, his big distraction was that – for the first time in his almost eight years – he had learned how to blow bubbles. Colleen had put mini champagne bottles filled with bubbles on every table. The plastic containers were small enough for her stepson to use. Gripping them in his hands, Little B never tired of dipping a wand in and out, before bringing it close to his eyes to check it was filled with soapy liquid and blowing. He didn't even abandon his new favourite pastime when Rhiannon Wolfe, a singer the couple had hired, started the evening reception with some classic rock hits. Everyone gathered around to listen and Little B wheeled his walker closer so that he could sway his lower body in time to the music while he blew even more bubbles.

Later, after Will and Colleen's first dance, Owen danced in their arms to the one song he'd personally requested, 'I Gotta Feeling' by the Black Eyed Peas, singing along to the lines, 'I gotta feeling that tonight's gonna be a good night!'

Then, to everyone's surprise, the music stopped and Little B's grandfather Bill Howkins took to the stage with a guitar and a microphone as Will stepped up to explain. 'There has been a long tradition in my family of Dad writing and performing a song at family occasions,' he told the bemused guests as he stood nervously at the front of the crowd. 'Now it's my turn!'

While family and friends looked on, Bill – who plays in a pub band for fun – struck up the first few chords and launched into a number recounting his son's love of fast food. It began: *'Now listen to my story, it is often really sad. It starts right off in Haslemere with the birth of a little lad. His life was oft not easy, he struggled in the fight, till a Kiwi (lass) she came along and damn sure put him right.'*

There were nine similar verses and a catchy chorus, which everyone soon sang along to. The final verse concluded: *'Now listen to a little secret of how he wooed Colleen. To let her know he fancied her and then to keep her keen. He took her in his mighty arms but the words he couldn't find. So Willy whispered tenderly the first thing on his mind. And as he felt her beating heart and the heaving of her breast, it felt so warm and comforting he there and then confessed: Your golden hair is beautiful and I love your crystal eyes. By the warmth of your chest I can tell you're blessed with a couple of meaty pies!'*

Bill then launched into the final chorus as everyone joined in: '*Ginsters pasties, Ginsters pies. With a bottle of Coke and Walker's crisps, they kept young Will alive. From Kosovo to Kabul they put him to the test, but Will survived with a couple of pies and a pasty up his vest!'*

Colleen's only objection to the song was one of Bill's final verses that went: '*Now we wish you well our William and Colleen, may you be blessed. And Owen lad you've a mighty dad – he really is the best. And should you wish to grow up like daddy big and wise, don't eat broad beans, any veggies, any greens, just go for the pasties and the pies.'*

As his grandfather sang those words and Colleen shook her head in disbelief, Owen punched the air with his tiny fist and cried, 'Yesss!!'

Staying up way past his normal bedtime seemed to give Little B renewed vigour. Not long after the music ended and he'd blown the last of his bubbles over Will and Colleen on the dance floor, he challenged all-comers to some arm-wrestling, at which he is naturally adept, thanks to his pronounced muscles. Propped up on a cushion, his dress shirt rolled back to his bicep, he cried 'Next!' as everyone from diminutive ladies to burly RAF crew fell to his prowess. During one game of best of three, and after he had – in his own words – 'trounced' a bomb disposal officer at his first arm-wrestling attempt, Owen grinned at him cheekily and asked, 'Any last words?'

When Jodi Kennedy was defeated, Little B quickly drew her a giant X on an iPad drawing app he had open on the table next to him.

'Oh, is that a kiss for me?' she asked, somewhat appeased.

'No. It means loser!' he replied, as her face fell.

Needless to say, his winning streak remained unbroken.

One of the last to leave with Will and Colleen, Owen could hardly keep his eyes open as his father carried his little man out to a waiting taxi. Suddenly, someone sitting outside the mill house spotted them leaving and cried out: 'Hey! That's the kid off the telly, isn't it? He's famous!'

'Yes he is!' Colleen replied proudly.

The fan quickly rushed over and asked for Owen's autograph. Mustering a sleepy smile, Little B said, 'You'll have to be quick. I'm very tired,' before graciously signing his name.

The new little family finally headed home to a waiting Haatchi after a day that had been full of tears and laughter. Mr and Mrs Will Howkins-Drummond, exhausted but happy, took Little B back to the home they'd created together, thankful for their many blessings.

9

'Keep your face to the sunshine and you cannot see a shadow.'

Helen Keller

AFTER ALL THE joy and excitement of their wedding, Will and Colleen spent a week at home in order to relish their bridal flowers, open all their cards, and have time with Aunt Tui and the Kennedys, who had come so far to see them. Little B's eighth birthday was also looming and they wanted to celebrate the build-up to it with him before they went away.

The only cloud on their horizon was the latest news about Owen's hips. Two days before their honeymoon began, Will and Colleen had to take him back to Southampton Hospital for the steroid injections that doctors hoped would ease his hip pain. Before Owen left home for the procedure, Haatchi gave him extra-special cuddles and a 'bravery booster' – lifting his front paw and pulling Little B to him in an embrace, so that their heads were pressed together and they were looking into each other's eyes. It was as if Haatchi was reassuring him that everything would be all right.

Once Owen was under anaesthetic (cuddling a favourite soft white bear that reminded him of Haatchi), his doctors were able to administer a cortisone injection into his left hip and then examine him more closely. He came round after the operation without incident and had no recollection of what had happened; nor did he appear to be in too much pain.

Taken to a children's ward to recover, he was tended by Colleen until a nurse came to remove the two cannulas, or plastic tubes, that had been inserted into the veins in his arm in order to administer the drugs. Knowing that he had to 'man up', Owen asked if he could remove the sticking plasters himself, so Colleen and the nurse soaked them in water in the hope that they wouldn't hurt quite so much when he peeled them off. Unfortunately that didn't work, so they had no choice but to rip them off in the end.

When it came to removing the tubes, Little B looked at Colleen fearfully and told her, 'I really wish this didn't have to happen today.' Squeezing his hand, she told him she really wished it didn't too.

Looking around the room at the other children lying quietly in their beds, Owen took his new stepmother firmly by the hand and told her, 'Can you please put your hand over my mouth if I scream, so that it doesn't upset the other children?' As his eyes filled with tears in anticipation of the pain, it was all she could do to stop herself from crying too.

When the nurse finally removed the cannulas, Owen couldn't stop himself from screaming. Colleen tried to distract him, making Red Indian noises by taking her hand on and off his mouth, and then it was over. Within a few minutes, he was sitting up in bed playing a favourite computer game. He was so distracted by it that when they asked him if he would like a bath to scrub off the pen marks on his legs before he went home, he replied: 'I'm in the middle of a war at the moment, so I can't help you.'

While Owen carried on playing with his machine, Will and Colleen met with the medical staff who had examined him under anaesthetic. Although they'd discovered that his left hip wasn't quite as damaged as they'd first thought, the top of each femur was severely flattened and deformed. They confirmed that one hip had worn a groove into Owen's pelvis as his tightening muscles had pulled it against the bone.

The right hip joint was dislocated by as much as two inches away from the socket and was off to one side. They said it had been pulled too far apart ever to be repositioned.

Belen Carsi, the paediatric orthopaedic specialist who talked the family through the results, admitted that the news was not good. 'Both hips were completely out of their sockets,' she said. 'The morphology of the bone had destroyed the head and the socket in such a way that they were not reconstructable. Furthermore, the part of the pelvis that had been ground away by the hip was now dead bone.'

This worrying development meant that there would be little point in surgeons replacing Owen's hip joints as they'd planned, as the new joints would simply dislocate clear of the sockets again. The doctors had also been unable to check on the vital blood flow to the bones because Little B's muscles were pulled too tight to allow them enough access to the arteries.

The surgeons explained that if the steroid injections didn't help Owen and he was still in pain, their only other option would be to cut two to three inches off the top of his leg bones to stop them from being ground against his other bones and wearing down. This would mean that he would almost certainly be permanently confined to a wheelchair, because there wouldn't be enough bone left in his legs to support his weight – especially as he grew bigger and heavier.

Belen Carsi said that the operation they were suggesting was more commonly done in patients with cerebral palsy, but even then it had only a 50 per cent success rate. The decision has to be based on quality of life, she added.

The news came as a major shock.

Although most people saw Owen in a wheelchair when he was out in public, at home he either used his walker to get around or manoeuvred himself between the furniture using chairs and tables for support. The independence this allowed him was vital to his morale, as he could take himself off to his bedroom, the bathroom or to hug Haatchi without assistance.

Ever the optimist, and also an engineer, Will began to try to think of ways in which his son's hips might be fixed. He wondered about the possible use of resorbable surgical mesh, sometimes known as scaffolding, which is used in tendon surgery. Once in place, the tendons are allowed to grow around the graft of polymer fibres.

He started drawing diagrams and playing around with models made of golf balls inside segmented tennis balls to see if he could work out some sort of innovative engineering solution using the latest technologies. He read up on the difference between ceramic and titanium joints.

After hours of pondering, he eventually came up with an idea for a custom-made curved 'extension' to Owen's pelvic sockets that he hoped could be screwed into place to create a mechanical lock for his hip joints. His design would allow Little B to walk, although not to move his leg sideways or upwards – but then he couldn't do that anyway.

Once he had the shape clear in his mind, Will began to make enquiries about the possibility of patenting his new invention. He also decided to seek out the advice of the world's leading orthopaedic surgeons, and especially that of the specialists in Boston and Baltimore who'd treated Ben Elwy when he'd had a similar problem at around the same age as Owen.

When Ben had a few inches removed from the tops of his legs at eight years old, his parents' greatest fear was that he wouldn't be able to use his walker, but that never happened. He is still scheduled to have his hips replaced when he reaches sixteen.

Will hoped to avoid that surgery for his son because of his new idea. Being so proactive was the only way he could think of to get past the fear that Little B might never walk again.

Determined to make the most of Owen's eighth birthday, the couple threw him a small party for friends and family, including Tui and Kathryn, Jodi and Peter, and they all watched as he opened his presents and cards. His new Nerf guns from Will and Colleen, with automatic triggers which were easier for his hands to use, were big hits, along with some Lego, a hover target and laser gun, and a set of bocce balls just like those he'd watched at the Paralympics with his dad.

Later on, Will took photos of him dressed up like an alien with a space-age helmet and full Nerf kit, and posted it with the caption: '*(Places head in hands and sighs) That will teach me for telling Owen he can wear whatever he likes at his next hospital appointment . . .*' On his personal web page, Will also posted a photo of Owen as a smiling two-year-old and wrote: '*Eight years ago was the proudest day of my life. Almost every day he makes me laugh and keeps me on my toes. I couldn't wish for a better son. Happy birthday Owen. Love you loads.*'

Only when Owen's birthday had been properly celebrated and their foreign visitors had finally flown home did Will and Colleen open all their wedding-day cards to see how much they'd managed to raise for their surprise trip to Lapland with Little B in December. They needed at least £5,000 for the flights, accommodation and

Owen's special requirements over four days, and they were delighted to find that, thanks to the generosity of their friends and family, they had almost half. They placed a deposit on the holiday and spoke to the travel company, Magic of Lapland, about what Little B would need. The staff couldn't have been more helpful, offering to let the family have a chalet of their own on the reindeer farm rather than staying at a nearby hotel with everyone else, to avoid having to move Owen around too much. They were fine about the oxygen too, and offered to provide special facilities so that Little B could still go mush with the dog team and take part in the snowmobile safari like all the other children. Owen's stiffening joints suffer badly in the cold, so he would need to be kept warm at all times, and the company promised they would provide thermal clothing for them all.

The couple planned on keeping it a surprise from Owen right up until they got him aboard the plane. They just looked forward to seeing his face when he finally set eyes on Father Christmas. They could hardly wait.

With everything set for their next big family adventure, Will and Colleen left Little B in the capable care of Kim's parents, Sara and Hugh, and finally headed to Scotland in the August sunshine for what proved to be a blissful week. It may not have been the Costa Rican tree house they'd originally dreamed of, but their honeymoon was all that Will and Colleen hoped it would be, and more. They had great weather, Haatchi and Mr Pixel thrived in the open spaces, and the couple could finally unwind.

In the wilds of Scotland, they were able to put any concerns about Owen's future from their minds for a few days and just enjoy the serenity of their idyllic honeymoon destination. Walking, reading and catching up on their sleep after a manic few months, they took in the incredible views, spotting rare birds and even a sea otter in the estuary next to their pretty white cottage, which they soon dubbed 'Haatchi's Hideaway'.

When a herd of curious Highland cattle turned up on their doorstep, they posted on behalf of their big tri-paw: 'I'm loving the Scottish raw-food delivery service. BOL!' In another post, Haatchi offered to taste-test the breakfast Will was cooking for Colleen, while Jan Wolfe, who ran the holiday cottages, proudly posted that they had a 'canine celebrity' in their midst.

Haatchi's hydrotherapy continued daily, with swims in the clear, cool water of the loch alongside a happy Mr Pixel, who chased balls and sticks until he could swim no more. Haatchi also managed some walking on the soft grass without his harness and was delighted to be able to move freely.

Their honeymoon ended all too soon and on their way home, halfway down the M6 and stuck in a traffic jam, they were sorely tempted to turn the car around and head back. 'The place was perfect in every way,' said Will, 'and we'd probably never have found it without Jan becoming a friend to Haatchi online, so that's yet another thing we owe him for.'

After returning to an empty house, they called Owen straight away and he assured them he was having a great time in Devon with his grandparents and Auntie Katie. He'd been to the local arcade and enjoyed a family barbecue, but mostly he was looking forward to his mother returning from Afghanistan after her three-month tour. Kim's whole family was driving Owen to RAF Brize Norton as a surprise to meet her. Although Little B had Skyped his mum often and been able to leave her messages any time he wanted, he couldn't wait to show her his new watch and tell her all his news. She in turn was excited to tell him that she'd managed to raise the equivalent of more than £2,000 among her colleagues in Afghanistan for his new Zippie wheelchair and that they were nearing their target.

Haatchi was improving daily after his Scottish holiday and was booked in for some more hydrotherapy and treadmill work to continue to strengthen his leg. His team of carers at Greyfriars and elsewhere devised an outdoor obstacle course for him, which could be set up at home to keep him agile and flexible even as the weather got colder. Like Owen, the big dog feels the cold, and winter isn't the best time for either of them, so keeping them warm and mobile is important.

Andy Moores, Haatchi's surgeon, continued to be impressed by the fact that not only had Haatchi been so cruelly treated in the past, but he had also had a huge amount of veterinary treatment in his life – yet he was always so incredibly placid. A lot of dogs who have been caged or restricted for long periods, or had pain inflicted on them by surgery, become difficult and aggressive. Haatchi, however, had tolerated it all with such grace that for Andy he was the perfect patient.

Which is why it was so surprising when gentle Haatchi took against one of the people he periodically came into contact with for therapy – a kind-hearted middle-aged man who loved animals and had been eager to meet the famous dog. Haatchi barked and growled very aggressively every time he saw the poor man, who was devastated at his reaction. Nobody could understand why, but then Colleen realized that, with his dark hair and olive skin, he probably looked a little like the man who'd been seen near the railway line where Haatchi was found. 'They say elephants never forget,' said Colleen, 'but clearly Anatolian Shepherds don't either.'

When Colleen returned to work, she began training for the 2014 London Marathon, which she had decided to run in aid of the White Lodge Centre in Chertsey, which supports the disabled and offers respite care to their families and carers and especially helps Alfie – the young son of a friend of hers – who has cerebral palsy.

Haatchi went back to hydrotherapy and was well enough to work again as a PAT dog. Owen – whose hips were still painful despite his injection – had further ordeals to face. He started a new term at school and underwent some more studies. His doctors were concerned about his sleep apnoea, which had worsened to the point that it was blocking his airway and interrupting his night-time breathing. Ear, nose, and throat specialists also warned that he might have to start wearing a full face mask at night as well as being fed nasally with oxygen. Will could only hope that his brave little boy would cope with a new contraption.

The honeymoon was well and truly over for Will and Colleen, and the normality of being a dad and stepmum returned to their lives with Haatchi and Little B. Not that any one of them was complaining.

'I didn't think I could love Little B any more than I already did,' said Colleen, 'but having Will's ring on my finger really made a difference somehow. When Owen came back to us from his mum's, I smothered him in kisses while he giggled and wriggled. We were so happy to have him home and we couldn't wait to start the next phase of our lives together as a family.'

They couldn't foresee the future for any one of them, and they knew there were many trials yet to face ahead, especially with Haatchi and Little B. But what Will and Colleen did know was that they were just so heart-swellingly grateful to have found one another and helped each other to find happiness, acceptance and – most of all – love.

After such an unhappy beginning for them all, the family hoped and prayed that they had found their happy ending.

Epilogue

*L*IFTING HIS HEAD, *he sniffed the air with his wet black nose. He thought he heard a noise but wasn't sure what it was so he slumped back down where he lay. Peering right and left through amber eyes, he wondered where his humans had gone and why he was alone in the dark.*

Would someone come soon?

He heard another noise and his tail stump twitched. It was coming from Owen's room. Then the overhead light flicked on. Through the cage of his special bedroom built into the dining room of his forever home, he could see his beloved mum approaching in her pink fluffy dressing gown. Behind her was his dad, wearing his airforce-blue pyjamas. In his arms he was carrying the most special human being in Haatchi's life – his very own Little B.

It was an ordinary Monday morning in the Howkins-Drummond household and all three humans had just woken up, ready to face their day. Owen was off to school as usual, Colleen would soon be heading out to work, and Will would be in and out but mostly at home with him and Mr Pixel.

Before they even put the kettle on or took a shower, though, they all emerged sleepily from their bedrooms and stumbled, yawning, towards where the huge Anatolian Shepherd spent his nights. They opened up the door of the bedroom that kept him safe from further injury and then one by one they crawled inside for a family hug, burying their faces in his soft fur.

Thrilled to see them all, Haatchi licked and snuggled and made joyful gurgling noises as his stump wiggled with excitement. Panting hot doggy breath and groaning with pleasure, the nine-stone dog eventually pulled himself to his full four-foot height to tower over eight-year-old Owen, the little boy whose life he had transformed.

'Haatchi's smiling!' Owen cried, as he peered up into the furry face of his best buddy. 'Good boy!'

Looking down and squinting through his glasses at the assorted toys on Haatchi's bed, Owen then picked up his favourite and held it out to the gentle giant like an offering. The dog carefully lifted Harold Hedgehog from Owen's tiny cramped hands in jaws powerful enough to snap the neck of a lion. Settling back down on to his bedding, Haatchi held the fluffy toy softly in his mouth, then dropped it and nudged it playfully towards Little B, cocking his head, hopeful for a game.

Colleen and Will curled up together in a comfy corner of the cage and watched happily as Owen took up the challenge and a playful tug-of-war began between a dog and his boy.

Haatchi had been in their lives for only two years, and yet it seemed as if he had always been a part of it. His gracious-ness and forgiveness astounded them daily, but they also knew that since the night he had fallen victim to the most terrible cruelty, he had experienced nothing but the milk of human kindness.

Everyone, from Nigel the rail manager and Siobhan the RSPCA inspector who together rescued him that bitterly cold night, all the way through to Stan, Fiona, Andy, Angela and all the veterinary staff who had cared for him, plus the numerous other volunteers who went out of their way to help, had led him to their door and – more especially – to Owen.

Both the dog and the boy had a long and arduous road ahead of them, but – together – it seemed as if they could take on the world. Rolling around in one giant ball of fur and love, it was almost impossible to see where Haatchi ended and Little B began.

As Will and Colleen wondered if they'd ever get Owen off to school that morning, Haatchi spoke to them in his special doggy talk and their courageous little boy erupted into one of his Woody Woodpecker giggling fits. Helpless against the mirth, the couple could do nothing but throw back their heads and laugh.

The World According to Haatchi and Little B

Baldy bot-bot	Haatchi's shaved leg and bottom after his surgery
BOL	Bark Out Loud (the canine equivalent of Laugh Out Loud, or LOL)
Boy-fur-iend	a male dog who is a friend of Haatchi's
Bravery booster	special cuddles between Haatchi and Little B for extra courage
Doggy doctor	the vet
Everypawdy	Haatchi's way of saying 'everybody'
Forever home	the home Haatchi now has for ever
Friday face	the happy face of Little B and Haatchi anticipating a weekend together

Girl-fur-iend	a female dog who is a friend of Haatchi's
Haatchi-handsome sleep	doggy beauty sleep
Haatchi-happyday	every day for Haatchi (except on a doggy doctor day)
Haatchi-love	what Haatchi has for everypawdy
Haatchi therapy	what Haatchi offers those in need
Haatch-Patch	nickname for Haatchi
Holibobs	holidays
Huggles	Haatchi hugs
Kiss-a-Freckle Friday	Fridays on Facebook featuring close-ups of Haatchi's freckly nose
Meet & Greet Brigade	Haatchi and Mr Pixel waiting in the window for Owen
Monday face	the sad face of Haatchi and Little B as he goes back to school
Nose art	the marks left on the window by Haatchi and Mr Pixel
Neighbourhood watch	Haatchi keeping watch for Owen and any wolves
OMD	Oh My Dog!
Ouch ouch	the name given to any pain felt by Haatchi or Little B
PAT	Pets As Therapy
Roly-poly grubadub	rolling in mud or water, best just after being groomed

Saturday sofa-surf	Haatchi and Little B's perfect weekend activity
Sleep Slug	a name for Little B, especially first thing in the morning
Sofa Spuds	nickname for Haatchi and Little B when they take root on the sofa
Snuggle Pup	Haatchi in full snuggle mode
Snuggle Bunnies	Haatchi and Little B snuggling together
Sprollie	Collie-Spaniel cross, a.k.a. Mr Pixel
Three-legged Fluff Monster	Haatchi in shedding mode
Three-legged Angel	Haatchi on his best behaviour
Throwback Thursday	the day for an old photograph on Facebook
Thumbs-up Tuesday	Owen giving the thumbs-up about something good
Tongue bath	Haatchi's personal grooming routine
Triple Trouble	Owen, Haatchi and Mr Pixel together
Wee Heartie	Little B most of the time
Wooftastic	Haatchi's expression for something that's made him happy
Woofy muchly	thanks very much

Acknowledgements

There are so many people to thank for helping Haatchi and Little B, some of whom we have never met. They include the train driver who first reported Haatchi on the tracks and Nigel Morris, the railway operations manager who helped lift him to safety and came to meet him recently.

Then there are all the animal and human doctors and therapists who have fought so valiantly to keep both Owen and Haatchi healthy and pain-free. We only hope that we have acknowledged you sufficiently within the pages of this book.

There are also those who have supported us more recently, especially our editor Doug Young and his team at Transworld Publishers, who fell in love with this story from the start and pulled out all the stops in order to be the ones to share it with the rest of the world. We would also like to thank publicist Polly Osborn for her infectious enthusiasm, and everyone from the people who designed and marketed this book to those who sell it in their shops.

The love and support of our families along every step of our journey with Haatchi and Little B have been invaluable, and we owe heartfelt thanks to our parents and parents-in-law Joan and Bill Howkins, Sara and Hugh Knott, and Kathryn and Tui Harrison, along with our brothers and sisters, friends and family.

A special note of thanks goes to Kim, Owen's mother, for generously supporting him and us in this project too.

We are indebted to you all.

Haatchi's life would never have been saved and then eased if it wasn't for the remarkable network of amazingly kind and generous animal lovers who helped him along the way. Little B has been similarly blessed.

Many of the people who have helped them both work voluntarily for charities that are in desperate need of support. Others are companies or organizations that would welcome your business in these hard-pressed times. If you would like to thank them in any way on behalf of Haatchi and Little B, then they (and we) would be delighted.

Their names and details are on the opposite page.

Woofy muchly!

All Dogs Matter
30 Aylmer Parade
London N2 0PE

Anderson Moores Vets
The Granary
Bunstead Farm
Poles Lane
Hursley
Winchester
Hampshire SO21 2LL

Crufts
www.crufts.org.uk

Dogs and Kisses
www.dogsandkisses.co.uk

Dogs Today Magazine
www.dogstodaymagazine.co.uk

Dogs Trust
www.dogstrust.org.uk

Endal Awards
www.londonpetshow.co.uk

Fiona Simpson Doggiebears
www.facebook.com/pages/The-papier-mache-zoo/
176374135774959

**Greyfriars Veterinary Rehabilitation & Hydrotherapy
Referrals**
The Veterinary Centre
Hogs Back
Guildford
Surrey GU3 1AG

Harmsworth Memorial Hospital
22 Sonderburg Road
Holloway
London N7 7QD

K9 Rehabilitation
2 Titchener Close
Bicester
Oxfordshire OX26 2BZ

Make A Wish Foundation
329–331 London Road
Camberley
Surrey GU15 3HQ

Muffin's Dream Foundation
www.muffinsdreamfoundation.co.uk

Nutriment Raw
Enterprise House
1 Bridge Road
Camberley
Surrey GU15 2QR

OrthoPets Europe
Elmtree House
Breadstone
Berkeley
Gloucestershire GL13 9HF

Petplan
Great West House
Brentford
Middlesex TW8 9DX

Rescue Helpers Unite
www.rescuehelpersunite.co.uk

RSPCA
Freepost (SW2465)
Horsham
West Sussex RH13 9RS

Sara Abbott Animal Portraits
www.sara-abbott.com

Starlight Children's Foundation
Macmillan House
Paddington Station
London W2 1HD
www.starlight.org.uk

UK German Shepherd Dog Rescue Ltd
3 Ash Lane
Appleton
Warrington
Cheshire WA4 3DD

White Lodge Centre
Holloway Hill
Chertsey
Surrey KT16 0AE

Picture Acknowledgements

All images have been supplied courtesy of the Howkins family except for the following:

Page 3: On the sofa of *This Morning* © ITV; winning 'Friends for Life' at Crufts © Crufts. Page 5: Haatchi's X-rays and the first day on his paws, both courtesy of Anderson Moores. Page 6: Winners of the Braveheart Award © The British Animal Honours 2013: Whizz Kid Productions Limited for ITV. Pages 7 and 8: Wedding photographs © Kenga photography.

Every effort has been made to trace copyright holders. We apologize for any omissions in this respect and will be pleased to make the appropriate acknowledgements in future editions.

ABOUT THE AUTHOR

Wendy Holden is an experienced author with two novels and thirty non-fiction books to her credit. She also wrote the bestselling memoir of Uggie, the dog from *The Artist*. Her ghosted autobiographies mostly chronicle the lives of extraordinary women, including the actress Goldie Hawn; a World War II spy; Frank Sinatra's widow Barbara; and the only woman in the French Foreign Legion. A former journalist for the *Daily Telegraph*, Wendy covered news events around the world and now lives in Suffolk, England, with her husband and two dogs.

Author's Note: For our American friends, here is a list of some of the animal advocates and children's charities that are great resources in the States and could do with your support.

HAATCHI & LITTLE B:
American Animal Advocacy and Children's Organizations

American Society for the Prevention of Cruelty to Animals (ASPCA)
424 East 92nd Street
New York, NY 10128
212-876-7700
http://www.aspca.org

Believe In Tomorrow Children's Foundation
6601 Frederick Road
Baltimore, MD 21228
800-933-5470
http://www.believeintomorrow.org

Best Friends Animal Society
5001 Angel Canyon Road
Kanab, UT 84741
435-644-2001
http://www.bestfriends.org

Children's Miracle Network Hospitals
205 West 700 South
Salt Lake City, Utah 84101
801-214-7400
http://www.childrensmiraclenetworkhospitals.org

Doris Day Animal League
2100 L Street NW
Washington, DC 20037
202-452-1100
http://www.ddal.org

The Humane Society of the United States
2100 L Street NW
Washington, DC 20037
202-452-1100
http://www.humanesociety.org

International Fund for Animal Welfare
290 Summer Street
Yarmouth Port, MA 02675
508-744-2000
http://www.ifaw.org

The MAGIC Foundation
6645 West North Avenue
Oak Park, IL 60302
800-362-4423
http://www.magicfoundation.org

Make-A-Wish International
4742 North 24th Street, Suite 400
Phoenix, AZ 85016
602-230-9900
http://worldwish.org

Mayo Clinic
Medical Genetics in Minnesota
200 First Street SW
Rochester, MN 55905
507-284-2511
http://www.mayoclinic.org

Medical Missions for Children, Inc.
35 Getty Avenue, Building 400
Paterson, NJ 07503
973-754-4971
http://www.mmissions.org

National Organization for Rare Disorders
55 Kenosia Avenue
Danbury, CT 06810
203-744-0100
https://www.rarediseases.org

North Shore Animal League America
25 Davis Avenue
Port Washington, NY 11050
516-883-7575
http://www.animalleague.org

Petfinder Foundation
4729 East Sunrise Drive, #119
Tucson, AZ 85718
520-207-0626
http://www.petfinderfoundation.com

St. Jude Children's Research Hospital
262 Danny Thomas Place
Memphis, TN 38105
http://www.stjude.org/

Shriners Hospitals for Children
http://www.shrinershospitalsforchildren.org

Starlight Children's Foundation
2049 Century Park East, Suite 4320
Los Angeles, CA 90067
310-479-1212
https://www.starlight.org